Accounting

A Comprehensive Guide for Beginners Who Want to Learn About Basic Accounting Principles, Small Business Taxes, and Bookkeeping Requirements

Contents

Introduction

This book discusses the core concepts and basics of accounting, providing you with a balance of theory and practical examples. Accounting is a vast concept with a wide range of uses, and if you run your own small business, knowledge of accounting and bookkeeping will give you the edge. Most accountants have expert-level knowledge, which allows them to provide top-level consulting services. Whether you have an accountant and want to learn more about it, or you're just starting in business and need to learn how to do it yourself, this book has you covered.

We cover the relevant tools, techniques, and methods used by today's accountants. Given that bookkeeping and accounting are primarily digitized now, we have ensured that the information is streamlined to the new technological techniques rather than outdated manual techniques.

From explaining the Chart of Accounts to the more creative ways to set up your accounting systems, we have made sure that you understand the full extent of the automated tasks while keeping the core ideas of accounting and other principles intact. The successful approach to running your business is to have people who perform these tasks but, we remembered business owners who can't afford to hire an accountant or consult one because of the high cost of a consultation.

Think of this guide as a "first-aid" guide to bookkeeping and accounting. Refer to it when you need help on the basic accounting principles, need to brush up on your skills, or even if you want to check up on what your bookkeeper or accountant is doing.

And discussing financial analysis tools and methods, we also cover taxation and its importance to business performance.

This book differs from all the other similar books on the market because we have taken the time to write it in an easy-to-read manner and explain any necessary jargon. So, if you are ready to take your first steps into accounting and bookkeeping, let's dive in.

Chapter 1: What is Accounting (and Can I Do It on My Own)?

Is accounting rocket science?

Will I be able to run my business without an accountant?

These are a few of the main questions you might ask yourself when running a business or considering becoming an accountant yourself. What do you think an accountant is, and what is the main idea or concept behind accounting?

To start, let's use a typical life example to illustrate that we perform accounting in our everyday lives. For instance, we may have a limited budget for the week's groceries, and we have to decide where best to spend the money to get the most value. You have to decide if you need that expensive brand or a lower brand will do just as well. You also have to decide if you need everything you want or if you should just stick to the essentials this week. Another example would be purchasing a car or a house through a loan. You will often find yourself deciding whether to **apply for a loan from this bank** or **go to another, which** offers a lower interest rate and more facilities.

Whatever the situation, we are all exposed to the basic accounting principles every day, and your decisions are just a smaller version of those a business owner must make.

Those basic principles include:

- Gathering financial information from various sources.
- Considering all known factors before deciding.
- Deciding and evaluating it occasionally.

What is Accounting?

Fundamentally, you are acting as your own accountant in many life situations. This lets you sometimes choose or find a much better deal when facing shortfalls in your budget or simply when you prefer to make expenditure cuts when your cash flow is tight.

Accounting revolves not only around the concept of cash or monetary wealth, but it also revolves around other fundamental areas that involve:

- Risk analysis and risk management
- Opportunity cost and decision making
- Optimal solutions for various problems etc.

Thus, in simple terms, accounting is:

"THE ANALYSIS OF THE RETROSPECTIVE EVENTS MERGED WITH PRESENT VARIABLE FACTORS TO MAKE A REASONABLE ASSUMPTION/ EXPECTATION OR FORM FUTURE DECISIONS."

Although many people consider that accounting means recording past events, that is not the case. Accounting has a far broader scope in the real world, expanding to most sectors and horizons of world economies.

Does an Accountant Play a Vital Role?

The short answer is yes. Business accounting provides you, as the owner, with a detailed picture of your business. An accountant can help you track your income and expenditures, make sure you stay compliant with government and state legislation, taxes and provide you, your investors, and the government with financial information, helping you make the right business decisions.

But an accountant wears many hats, depending on the type and size of business they work for, such as:

Advice on Business Structures

One of the most critical accounting roles is giving advice, and much of that surrounds structuring your business in the right way. It also covers financial restructuring, corporate compliance, and these diverse areas:

- HR policies and employee enhancement programs
- Implementation of an efficient control system
- Organizational enhancement structures
- Mergers and Acquisitions
- Legal matters and dispute resolution, etc.

More accountants are also branching out into giving independent financial advice and business analysis.

Invoices and Billing

Every business's primary goal is to earn money. An accountant is needed to make sure every customer is billed and invoiced on a timely basis. If nobody is issuing invoices or recovering the money from customers, your business cannot succeed. An accountant is essential to oversee these processes and perform the necessary steps to handle these matters.

Credit Limits and Booking Sales

Businesses determine the credit limits of their customers, and these play a crucial role. **Credit limits decide how much the customer may take in goods or services rendered without paying right away.** Many businesses rely on working within their credit limits, as loans are a typical transaction when businesses are starting up. Sales are a vital part of the business's success, determining its growth and profitability potential. An accountant can easily keep a record of such sales for small businesses.

They provide a large variety of reports about small businesses, including customer reports determining who the major buyers are and who require frequent goods and services from you?

Supplier Invoices

An accountant's primary task is to manage the finances or manage the business's money to use it most optimally. Accountants do the particular phase of payments at the right time to make sure that a streamlined process is followed. Suppliers mostly contact the accountant of the business directly to ask about their outstanding invoices. It is the accountant's job to make sure that they are paid at the right time and that the company doesn't run out of cash. This is a vital function to keep business flowing smoothly.

Payroll System Management

In large businesses, HR handles the task of creating the payroll. In small businesses, the accountant mainly looks after the payroll and hiring as well. Accountants are needed to create the payroll to keep track of the employees so that no employee is overpaid or underpaid in any circumstances. If there are more than three to four employees in a business, it becomes difficult to keep track of all their payments - not to mention how much your business owes those employees. Accountants create a much-streamlined process that ensures time is recorded adequately, and no employee is left unpaid each month.

Legal Consultant

The laws of every country are continually changing, and this can lead to:

- Restriction in the performance of business activities
- Abiding by specific new rules and regulations to avoid penalties
- Evaluation of the on-going performance of business activities in the country

It is essentially a requirement to have an accountant represent you in legal matters because accountants are always up to date in their field of knowledge. This allows companies to avoid any restrictions or fines that can impair their business growth.

Do You Need an Accountant?

Small businesses rarely need an accountant to perform these tasks. It is not safe to assume that accountants are not needed, and many business owners and entrepreneurs have an accountant by their side to make sure their business runs smoothly.

When one person tries to do everything, it is too much, and the business will suffer. An accountant or bookkeeper might be needed to help with the workload while getting on with the daily business needs.

But if you are a small business owner and want to handle these aspects on a smaller scale, then your approach to handling these things on your own is feasible and cost-effective.

The key to this system is balancing your workload and making sure you don't take on too much. This will guarantee disruption is kept to a minimum, and the business can run smoothly.

Primary Tasks of an Accountant

To illustrate, please have a look at the following image:

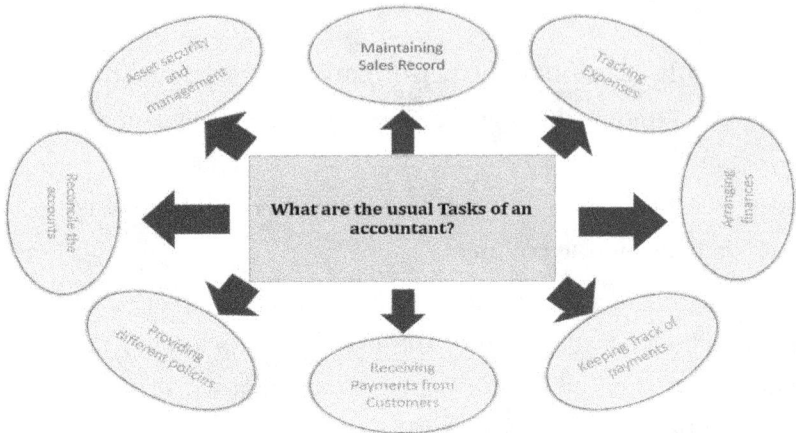

The image explains the crucial elements to help you get up to speed with what you must remember when you act as your accountant:

1. Have a proper sales record maintained.

2. Keep track of all your expenses and don't accidentally pay an invoice twice – this can happen with large businesses due to glitches in their accounting software.

3. Ensure that you have a solid policy in place and a proper contract that enforces customer payments within the timeline defined and gives no customer excessive credit. Have an appropriate credit limit for each customer and change it whenever necessary.

4. Ensure that you have proper contact with the bank so that if you ever run low on cash, the bank can provide a loan to cover the costs and keep your business going.

5. Play it safe when selecting your suppliers, as many people often place too much trust in a supplier, which they use to exploit their customers and increase their prices. So always look for different quotes and weigh them up before making a decision.

6. Make sure that security is in place to protect your valuables. This can include cash, vehicles, or high-value inventory, which can be easily pocketed or stolen.

Chapter 2: Accounting Vs. Bookkeeping

In the previous chapter, we learned about accounting and what being an accountant means. This chapter will unveil the common differences between accounting and bookkeeping, giving you a snapshot of what each handles.

Is Accounting Different from Bookkeeping?

You may come across these terms and think that accounting and bookkeeping are the same things, but we assure you they are not. To explain why, consider that bookkeeping is like a slice of a pizza, whereas accounting is the whole pizza.

Bookkeeping is a small slice of the larger pie, a small part of accounting, whereas accounting has a much more comprehensive and broader scope.

We can take this to another level. Accounting is summarized into five major components, and the following flowchart will provide a lot of value to your understanding.

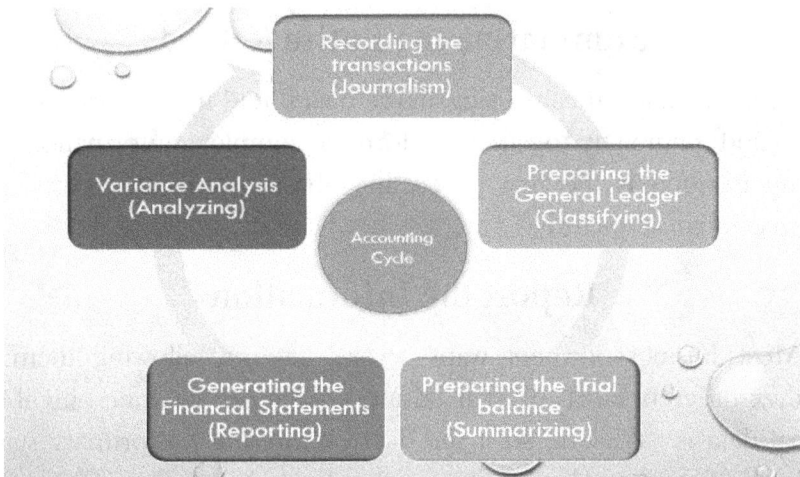

So here we can see that accounting combines its sub-divided components:

Record the Transactions

This component involves recording the financial transactions which have occurred. This is a crucial technique to ensure that all data is captured and considered for necessary processing. Every accountant ensures that the data or transaction, which they record, has all the necessary details and meets all the necessary criteria to prove the data's adequacy. This first step plays a significant role in three key areas:

a) An integrated control system that perfectly captures all required data.

b) Surety in the continuity of the business's financial strength.

c) Reporting at the final stage.

Classifying the Recorded Transactions

Once the data is captured and recorded, the next phase involves classifying those transactions into various headings, according to what the transaction pertains to. Examples include office furniture, business vehicle expenditure, stock, sales, and so on.

Summarize the Entire Record

Summarization means using all the data found in every category or class and putting it together to form a complete information set. Summarization is the first processing phase, displaying a brief but concise financial picture.

Report the Information

Most business owners want several reports, allowing them to analyze different facets of their business. That can be done only if the initial data is sufficient, so if the data captured at the primary stages lacked solid ground and detail, the final reports would not be complete. The most important report is the profit/loss statement, showing the business's financial standings quickly.

Analyze the Information

Even though the information may seem organized and easy to understand, it can be far from it. Much of this comes down to who collected and processed the information and how good the records were. If proper records are not kept, it may be impossible for a third-party, such as a bookkeeper, to understand them. Information analysis involves matching the information to previous years, providing an idea of whether the business has grown or not and how successfully, or otherwise.

10 Major Differences Between Bookkeeping and Accounting

To clarify the difference between the two, we have placed a side-by-side comparison table, illustrating this better.

	Accounting	Bookkeeping
Scope	We have elaborated on how it considers all five components to form a single scope in accounting. But its major work acts out on interpretation, analyzing, and reporting the financial information.	Bookkeeping is typically involved in the identification, measurement, and recording of financial events. That's why bookkeeping is a part of accounting.
Data Processing	Accounting involves heavily extensive data processing, as every single part of the data obtained has to be reported in a concise and meaningful manner.	There is no data processing in bookkeeping as it only captures the data, records it, and provides safekeeping of data collection.
Management's Decisions	Accounting is the primary tool used by the management for decision-making. Accounting is further divided into two main areas that include cost and management accounting and financial accounting. Management uses both of accounting for their respective uses and needs.	Bookkeeping doesn't allow management to form decisions or make valuable decisions based on the data gathered, as raw data provides no insight into how it reflects the overall process unless it is processed adequately.

Use in Purpose	Accounting's use or purpose is primarily for management and third parties to obtain valuable information about its operations.	Bookkeeping's use and purpose is to capture and record financial events adequately.
Competency Required	Accounting requires competent people to form reports, and analyzing the data is complex and complicated.	Bookkeeping doesn't require competency as it is followed in a systematic and pre-designed manner.
Categories	Accounting is further divided into categories for management use. (Explained above)	Bookkeeping is divided into two systems. Single-entry systems or dual entry systems.
Report Preparation	Various reports and financial statements are prepared at the end of the accounting procedure.	Bookkeeping doesn't involve the preparation of any such statements.
Analyze the Information	Accounting involves an extensive analysis of the information, which only well-trained people can do due to the complexity of the task's nature.	It includes no analysis of the information.

Qualifications	The necessary qualifications for a person to be a competent accountant include being either a CA (Chartered Accountant), ACCA (Association of Chartered Certified Accountant), CPA (Certified Public Accountant), CMA (Cost and Management Accountant), etc.	Any person can perform bookkeeping with any qualifications.
Level of Experience	Accounting requires a great level of experience.	Bookkeeping requires no experience as it is easy to perform.

Modern Day Bookkeeping and Accounting

In modern times, both fields have experienced massive changes and shifts in their scope and line of work. With introducing semi-automatic processing and AI (Artificial Intelligence), the world around accounting and bookkeeping quickly evolved to cope with ever-changing technology.

Experts estimate that the accounting business will be valued at almost $12 billion by 2026. Now, most small businesses and startups consider the accountant one of the most critical parts of their organization. That might seem like a surprising statistic, but the main factor in all this is that organizations realize the bookkeeper's importance, help a business streamline operations, and manage their finances. A good bookkeeper can make life a little easier for the accountant, allowing them to produce accurate reports at the right times to make sure of compliance and to process tax filings when due.

The Emergence of Accounting and Bookkeeping Software

The never-ending changes in technology led to the combination of both accounting and bookkeeping software and software such as QuickBooks, SAAP, and Sage50, which combined both processes. Once the data is entered and punched into the system, the software automatically displays all the reports, eliminating the effort to classify, summarize, and report data and go straight to recording the transactions and then receiving the desired reports. These reports also give a detailed analysis and review of the financial information.

Efficient and Economic Services

Due to these rapid changes, many services accountants traditionally offered became extraordinarily competitive and cheap. This made multiple services such as bookkeeping, tax preparation, and financial statement analysis cheaper to prepare when individually offered or even as a whole. As more consistency and integrity were found in the information that companies could produce, people didn't need help from accountants. The same set of information needed for official and governmental purposes was easily produced.

Financial Literacy and Ease in Processes

World modernization has led to more people being financially literate. Many people who used to find bookkeeping and accounting a difficult task now find it easier to adapt. These days, most retail stores, restaurants, even coffee shops' built-in integrated system takes the order and keeps track of the inventory and the sales made per order. This has led to more people being aware of the need to be financially literate and make the right business decisions to succeed.

Introduction of New Services

Remote working has never been easier. High-speed internet, cloud-based computing, and online databases have made it possible to work from just about anywhere globally, which has helped to introduce a new line of services offered by bookkeepers and accountants. A bookkeeper can work from anywhere, as they have access to decent internet, which has led to a surge in outsourcing. Business owners can now hire a bookkeeper online, using freelancer agencies, outsourcing agencies, and simple online advertising. Parts of the business easy to outsource include:

- Payroll processing systems and online payroll management systems

- Credit Card and Debit card processing systems

- Reconciliation of the financial transactions

- Tax calculation and tax-related services

- Internal control management systems, etc.

These services have allowed many companies and small businesses to increase their profitability and ease the processes. And freelancers can access the work from anywhere in the world.

Besides all this, even accountants have enhanced their level of services, including:

- Financial advisory and risk assessment advisory

- Budgeting and resource management

- Financial analyst and forecasting, etc.

The Future Reality of Bookkeeping and Accounting

After learning how bookkeeping and accounting have merged, you realize what the future holds in both fields. It is an unarguable fact that soon AI (Artificial Intelligence) will take over the entire process of bookkeeping and accounting. As machines automatically capture and record transactions, less human interaction will be involved in the entire process.

The most useful service, which will stay afloat regardless of AI introduction, will be financial analysis and resource allocation. Auditing will also stay in existence due to its regulatory status. Otherwise, bookkeeping will become obsolete shortly.

Key Tips to Select the Perfect Bookkeeping Software

When selecting the bookkeeping and accounting software, follow these essential tips:

1. Select the software that offers the perfect compatibility for your use. If you are a service industry, you select the software that offers the best accounting for service businesses.

2. Remember to stay consistent when inputting data into your systems, as it is an essential daily chore to follow.

3. Don't be afraid to change the software if you feel the current one doesn't fulfill your requirements.

4. Follow the key instructions and guidelines that come with each software so you can navigate better.

5. Remember to buy the software that offers security and protection against unauthorized entry, as your records are also precious and crucial to your business.

6. Keep a good habit of having several backups of the records and make sure you have an indexed physical record to navigate easily.

Chapter 3: Which Accounting Methods Suit My Small Business?

In the previous chapters, we explained the primary ideas and concepts about accounting and how it differs from bookkeeping. In this section, we will cover the following core ideas:

- The need for accounting methods and their essential types

- The crucial need for accounting methods in business entities

- Core benefits of each type of system. And most importantly

- How would this provide a direct benefit to you as a small business owner?

Do I Need an Accounting Method?

You may hear many accountants use the term "accounting methods" and wonder what accounting methods are? For the ease of your understanding, an accounting method is how you handle your accounts or financial records. Typically, financial records aren't the only things considered for accounting methods: non-financial records, events, or aspects can directly play in financial transactions. Don't worry about this, as this doesn't concern you. It is briefly defined here to elaborate on what can constitute a financial record.

You need an accounting method for your small business. You need this because:

1. Accounting methods create an easy way to identify the natural aspect of reporting your business.

2. It creates ease in understanding how your business performs with variable changing factors.

3. It allows your business to realize and recognize revenue and thus report accurate or adequate profits.

At this point, you may be wondering whether you need to decide upon an accounting method, but you may also wonder what all this means.

Accrual or Cash - What are These Accounting Methods?

Usually, the accounting methods are categorized into two:

1. Cash method of accounting

2. Accrual method of accounting

Cash Method

The cash method of accounting involves recording all the financial transactions based on the amount of cash received or cash spent during a particular period. This includes the cash received or spent in the form of banking transactions or cash in hand.

Small business owners mostly use the cash method of accounting, as it is easy to maintain and needs the physical cash to be present for use. For business taxes and preparation of the financial records, it is essential to remember that the primary selection of a method at the start can have huge risks or rewards associated with it.

To further elaborate, the Cash method of accounting states:

• **Recording Physical Income** - Say you received a sum of money from a client after a particular period. The income was received on the first day of the next calendar period but was associated with the previous calendar period. This income will be logged into the next calendar period.

• **Book Paid Expenses** - Say that the salaries of the employees in December 2018 were paid in January 2019. The expense would be recorded in January 2019.

Accrual Method

This method of accounting involves recording revenue with associated expenses or vice versa. This also means that revenue or expense related to a particular period must be recorded in the same period rather than recording when received or paid.

This method follows the accounting principle of the **Matching Concept** that states that:

• **Revenue - It must be recorded when we receive it.** For instance, you have supplied goods or services to a customer and sent an invoice in January 2019 but received the payment in February 2019. Here, your revenue must be logged in January 2019.

• **Expenses - Must be logged when we pay them.** For instance, salaries of the staff for January 2019 were paid in February 2019. As these salaries relate to January 2019, they should have been recorded at that time.

The Accrual accounting method follows a unique composure of accounting entries involving the right to receive, or a right to receive is established. Our revenue must be logged along with a corresponding asset, termed as a receivable.

The same case applies that when we must pay, or when it is established that we must pay for a service or goods received, we book our expenses and correspondingly book a liability, i.e., an obligation by the business to pay.

The fundamental idea of the matching concept leads many businesses to consider the accrual method of accounting.

5 Pros and Cons to Know Which Method Suits You the Best

Cash Method - Pros

The cash method has these pros:

1. Bookkeeping is Simple and Comparatively Easy

Maintaining your records based on cash is easy, and it keeps the records in a streamlined manner. The entire bookkeeping process becomes simple. There should never be any concern that income and expenses have not been included in the system, particularly those that should be logged. As everything will get reconciled at the end of a certain period, the idea that income or expenses will be missed or left unrecorded won't be an issue. It doesn't mean that invoices or bills won't be generated, as all bookkeeping records will eventually generate invoices or bills to display that these match with the cash received or spent.

2. Accurate Cash Flow Tracks

As everything is maintained in the form of cash at hand or cash in the bank, every point of the accounting system displays and tells you how much cash can be used and how much financing will be needed to sustain any future activity. This also provides the perfect indicator of the cash strength of a business.

3. Easy to Reconcile the Cash Using the Records

Not only that, but this method also allows business owners to reconcile any differences that arise during their work in a shorter period. Since transactions can be traced through the actual amount of cash, it makes the small business owner's work easy, especially if all cash transactions were recorded when they happened.

4. No Need for an Accountant or Advisor

With the immense flexibility and easy understanding of the method, there is no need for an expert-level accountant or advisor to be employed, thus saving money. You can easily perform the task of maintaining the records yourself and have it done relatively quickly, so long as you record everything regularly and don't leave it all to the end of the month.

5. Cost-Effective and Cheap to Sustain

The best advantage of the method is that it is extremely cost-effective. Along with that, this entire method saves time and resources to focus on more crucial work rather than having to spend countless hours fixing accounting records or errors.

Disadvantages

As with anything, there are always disadvantages that offset the benefits in different situations.

1. Unclear Picture About the Performance of the Business

This is one of the most significant downsides of the cash method. To show you what I mean, let me give you an example. For instance, your business performs its activities in the construction sector. You must have financing (a loan) to start the work before receiving the house's construction payments (after three years). If you go to a bank or any financial institution and ask for a loan, they will likely reject your application because you have not received a cash payment for doing the construction, and you have yet to record any revenue for the project. This is the case until the end of the project, and the bank will not consider this until the money is paid. Without finance or a loan, you won't be able to construct the house, and thus you will receive no revenue.

This example depicts the vicious cycle in which small business owners can get stuck while adopting the cash method. It creates an unclear image of business performance and the business's ability to continue. Not only that:\

- It shows the business's poor performance if the business earns revenue in a single season and not over a more extended period.

- It depicts that the business has immense losses when the significant financing or loans are eventually paid back to the financial institutions.

- It categorizes the business as high risk with high rewards, which many shareholders or investors are unwilling to take.

2. Disturbance in Tracking Profit Each Month

Another big drawback of this method is calculating the profit after the period. For instance, if you didn't pay the salaries or warehouse rent for a particular month, it would be difficult to know the actual profit for that month. Not only that, but this insecurity also makes it harder to perform any analysis.

3. Misreporting and Improper Basis for Comparison

This method relies heavily on when the cash is paid, creating a gateway for people to misuse and misreport the facts and figures. Typically, small business owners manipulate the figures by delaying payments or simply avoiding recording such payments as cash-in-hand transactions are the least likely to be well documented. This creates two major issues:

- This method is well known among investors, making them less likely to invest in your business if it follows such a method.

- A comparison of such records is impossible due to the volatile behavior that the business portrays.

4. Harder to Keep track of Receivables and Payables

Most businesses rely on credit terms, allowing them to manage their finances and cash flows better. In the cash accounting method, the concept of receivables and payables doesn't exist. That's why many small business owners have to keep a separate record of such transactions, which is harder to maintain and follow.

5. Inaccurate Forecasts

As many risks associated with the businesses involve revenue recognition and understatement of expenses, this causes inaccurate forecasts about the business's performance.

Pros in the Use of Accrual Method

Standard business practices include using the accrual accounting method because of the wide range of benefits.

1. More Optimized Track Record

The best pro-benefit of using the accrual method is that it tracks the operational performance much better. Recording all the transactions at the date of occurrence allows the business owner to analyze the business and its working conditions better.

2. Increase Third-Party Trust and Reliability

As the business creates a more unified and well-mannered form of reporting and financial statements, it increases its credibility. This allows third parties such as investors to invest in the business or banks to provide loans and finances and build a better client reputation and a diverse portfolio.

3. Accounting for Every Single Transaction

The best part about accrual-based accounting is that every aspect of the business is properly recorded, documented, and passed through the system to ensure everything is in order. Not only that, but it also gives the best idea about the receivables and payables of the business and is more transparent.

4. Accurate Profitability Each Month

The Accrual method of accounting provides accurate profitability margins at the end of each period or month-end. This makes the company perform monthly or periodic analysis by comparing the figures with the previous year to understand its performance.

In the earlier instance, it was described that for a construction sector business, the ability to take up loans is practically impossible while following the cash method. That issue gets resolved easily by the accrual method of accounting.

5. Easy Analysis and Forecasts

Many accountants can create well-designed reports and forecasts, which accurately depict the business's future in the upcoming months. Large entities have a highly skilled profile of expert accountants present in large numbers who constantly monitor and examine its growth in the forthcoming periods. It can also become easy for small businesses, as many factors are already available, and it can be easily forecasted whether the business will survive.

Cons of Accrual Method

Even though the accrual method may seem outstanding and the best to adopt, it also has cons, making it incompatible for certain people.

1. Difficult to Track Cash Flow Issues

All businesses need to understand the cash they have to use for various financial activities. Tracing cash flow is comparatively easy in the accrual method, but the problems within those said cash flows are hard to determine. The main reason is when the financial statements follow the accrual method, they consider non-cash items/ transactions and even those that haven't been cashed in or out. The best example of this is the same construction industry, which has taken a loan and based its activities on the accrual method. Now the company might be depicting hefty profits and incurring costs, but, in reality, there is no physical presence of cash, and their account could be standing at a zero balance.

2. It Can Be Expensive and Complex

The accrual method has a complicated design to follow to provide optimal results and reports. Since these designs have to be in place within a proper control system, it sometimes becomes expensive to maintain or sustain such designs. Larger companies and businesses' gigantic network integrates humans with machines to produce accurate and non-collusive results. These designs, which have to be in place, sometimes cost a lot of money and are so complicated they need consistent help from experts.

3. Stay up to Date with New Laws

One big issue about the accrual method is that all accountants or business owners must continuously stay in touch with new accounting standards and the new laws. You would need to know new accounting standards because they always affect the existing laws. All business owners need to understand and enforce them.

4. More Money Means More Tax

Let's take the same example of the construction industry business where the person is earning high profits due to adopting the accrual method. Since their financial statements show profits, they would have to pay taxes on the profit earned. From the previous example explanation, they don't have the money to pay tax as there has been no money received until now.

This is precisely why the accrual method makes people pay more taxes in one particular period and then fewer taxes in another. This makes it more complicated for business owners to understand how these tax laws affect their financial performance.

5. The Constant Need for an Expert

You will need an accountant's help often because working as an administrator or banker is an intensive routine. Not only that, but accountants will also only solve such matters they are trained to handle when dealing with complex or unknown issues or cases. Thus, this increases the cost of handling the accounts and the accrual method.

Which Method is Perfect for You?

Now the real question that arises – what accounting method will suit my company the best? You may have noticed that each method has pros and cons.

Here are ways to best relate to your situation, helping you choose the most suitable method for your business. For instance, if you are a small business owner and want to run an independent business with no accountants or you are a business accountant, the **cash method of accounting** would suit you the best. The reason is that:

    0• You may want to save costs and not have a large amount of time invested in accounting records or maintaining financial records. Or

    1• You may incur a cost, but your business direction or the business motive is to handle a more cash-based profit, so cash flow problems or reconciliations do not arise.

You can also adopt the accrual method based on the pros and cons you read in the last section. The method selection is weighted on three factors:

1. Business structure or business motive.

2. Resource utilization.

3. Reporting requirements.

Suppose your company follows a strict pattern or line where significant revenues are seasonal or period-based, or your company heavily relies on the reporting requirements to track business requirements better. There, the **accrual method** is perfect for your needs. As you know from the accrual method downsides, one of the main things to look out for is the cost and the necessity of such reports.

As a small business owner, you may not face such requirements of needing a high reporting line. Still, if you are a stable business and want to expand further, then the accrual method will depict your business's actual position and performance so it can expand further. Hence, if you start your business from the basics, adopt the cash method to ease the entire process.

Almost everywhere, regulatory bodies allow a business to shift from one method to another. The safe and secure approach uses both methods when you feel it is the right time to adopt that method.

Getting Into the Systems: Single Entry or Double Entry

The detailing of your chosen method gives you direction. Whether you want to perform record maintenance daily, weekly, or monthly, there is bound to be a method you can follow easily because, inherently, you will need to keep track of references before properly maintaining the financial records.

Suppose you are caught up in daily work and don't have time to compile all the transactions into proper records. What would be your approach to making sure that today's transactions aren't forgotten by tomorrow? You might typically note them down in a rough manner somewhere as a reminder. That is how the accounting systems work. They are based on the idea that the data written into the transaction's record is incomplete and written roughly – or written in full detail by reflecting on its appropriate nature.

Partial System: Single Entries

Just as the name describes it, it is a partial system. This system is only partial because it doesn't consider the level of accounting needed. Most transactions are maintained roughly or partially, with little information present about each transaction. This system is relatively easy and simple, but things get a little more difficult when processing it into the correct classes or groups.

A single-entry system primarily controls the cash received and the cash spent. It doesn't consider the inventory, the receivables, and the payables in the system. Remember that this system is not the perfect match for the cash method. Because many people maintain a single-entry system employing the accrual method, it facilitates performing control evaluations.

How Does this System Work?

This system works like a small cash statement. For instance, in a cash statement, there are two columns. In the right column, write the amount of cash and any other income received, while in the left column, write all the expenses and anything else that reduces our cash reserves. This is much like a personal record book that allows you to maintain partial information about each transaction. This is commonly done by many people when recording partial information in their checkbooks.

What this system doesn't correctly maintain is the *balance sheet information,* such as assets or liabilities. Many people use them as control measures to reassess their entire assets or liabilities under the accrual method. This approach is sometimes misleading and can lead to fraudulent activities taking place.

The General Accepted Accounting Principles (GAAP) don't recommend following the single-entry approach – even for small businesses – because of that very reason. Because it is easy to record transactions, many people opt to continue this to save time and resources.

The Complete System: Double Entry System

Almost every SME (Small Medium Enterprise) business and large businesses follow the modern world's double-entry accounting system. It is a popular method because it keeps the entire system of accounting well maintained and balanced. Common practices and principles are also based on the double-entry system because it provides a more secure and well-balanced approach to maintaining the accounts.

The main reason this system is so popular is that it prevents multiple errors and other mistakes from taking place and allows you to prevent common mistakes, which can sometimes become harder to detect.

How Does this System Perform?

This system's central concept is that every transaction has two effects, opposite to one another; there will always be an increasing impact while, simultaneously, there will also be a decreasing impact. Such impacts give an overall equilibrium, and the equation is always balanced. These two balancing natures of the transactions are called *debit* and *credit.*

The concepts regarding debit and credit may seem misguided. We can simplify the inaccurate accounting concept by saying that some account elements are debits, and some are credits. That's not to say that debit elements cannot also occur as a credit and vice versa.

We will not go into detail about the accounting equation here, but it is essential to explain it briefly to help you understand. We'll cover this more broadly in an upcoming chapter.

These natures of debit and credit fall into the direct criteria of the accounting equation, which is:

ASSETS = LIABILITIES + OWNER'S EQUITY

whereby

ASSETS (Debit nature) = LIABILITIES + OWNERS'S EQUITY (Credit nature)

From the equation, we can see that assets primarily have a debit nature while liabilities or owners' equity has a credit nature. Thus, whenever an asset (say the purchase of a vehicle occurred in this transaction) increases, this will be considered a debit. If it is caused by a liability (say a bank loan was taken, so the bank name should be titled in the transaction), then the credit effect becomes one of liability.

This entire transaction will be depicted like this:

Vehicle A/C (An Asset)   Dr. 10,000

To Bank Loan- BOA A/C (A Liability)   Cr. 10,000

This transaction reflects the equally balanced equation on the purchase of an asset with liability. If the reduction of another asset causes it (say you purchased the vehicle with cash in hand or cash at the bank), that asset will have an equal credit effect, reducing the asset.

For example:

Vehicle A/C (An Asset)   Dr. 10,000

To Cash at Bank A/C   Cr. 10,000

(The symbol A/C means account.) Here in these transactions, we have seen how debit and credit natures play a role in the double-entry accounting system, which is not found in the single-entry system.

Common Differences to Help You Understand Both Systems

To clear up any misconceptions or misunderstandings you may have, we will provide the differences between both systems, as follows.

- The impartial system of single entry only records one side of the transaction, a debit or a credit. The complete mechanism of the double-entry system records both effects for a balanced approach.

- The impartial system is relatively simple and easy to handle, whereas the double-entry system is comparatively harder to maintain and sometimes becomes complex to handle.

- The impartial system doesn't produce accurate and complete records, while the other system produces accurate and error-free results in most cases.

- It is easy to detect and trace any errors or risks of fraudulent activities in the double-entry system. In contrast, the impartial system offers no technique that can help trace fraudulent activities.

- The best and most accurate comparison of the two periods can be made only with the balanced system rather than the single-entry system. The latter doesn't provide a good record-maintenance technique.

In the following chapters, we'll focus on all techniques and learning methodologies in the double-entry system with the accrual method as this system is complex to handle. Unless specified, we will explain the cash method when working with the systems.

Chapter 4: Ten Tools for Digital Accounting

This section of the chapter will focus on accounting software and its need in modern times. Essentially this chapter will cover:

- The different types of accounting software and use in the technological era

- The key differences between various software

- The benefit various software will provide you with according to your business model

This chapter will typically cover the different software that businesses use. We will try to keep the information as relatable to you as possible.

Digital Software of the 21st Century

Ever since technology entered our lives, almost every single aspect of life has been transformed. Most technologies are designed to help us save time, making life simpler and more efficient. Most people embrace technology these days. Even in accounting, digital software has made remarkable breakthroughs, allowing millions of consumers to do their work more easily while dedicating time to their businesses' more crucial aspects.

Many current accounting software packages have hugely affected how large and small businesses can control their finances. The most common software packages popular among the small businesses are:

- QuickBooks Online
- Sage Accounting
- Xero
- Sage 300
- FreshBooks
- WagePoint
- SurePayroll
- TSheets
- Expensify
- Neat

Being an entrepreneur is challenging, and during these challenging times, it is also essential to manage your business efficiently. Trying to manage every aspect of your business is hard, especially for keeping track of your finances while ensuring everything else runs smoothly. Luckily, most accounting software makes life easier. While it won't do everything for you, it can take the brunt of the work, making it a real game-changer for almost every business.

1. QuickBooks Online

Starting with one of the most popular accounting tools, QuickBooks Online has emerged as a game-changing software that provided ease in the workplace. With simple invoicing to record handling and tracking payments, QuickBooks does it all while you sit back, relax, and enjoy a cup of coffee and watch your business boom in the market. Most business owners don't have the time to spend on their financial records to make sure their business runs smoothly.

Luckily QuickBooks Online saves you from much of the work and even produces reports on late-paying customers. And if you are worried that QuickBooks Online might not be adaptive to your business model, don't be because it has a vast range of built-in databases that suit many users.

QuickBooks also allows you to pre-load your custom invoice template rather than relying on standard designs in the system. With the considerable diversity in the reporting and the advanced reporting functionalities offered by QuickBooks, you won't have to invest time in preparing reports either.

With the automatic sync features, QuickBooks integrates your bank statements or credit card e-statements and processes them instantly. In short, QuickBooks help you manage just about every financial aspect of your business.

2. Sage Accounting

Following the same popularity as QuickBooks Online, Sage Accounting also benefits you and your company. This accounting software typically handles the project management features and other features related to particular jobs. By providing accurate costing and cost allocation to jobs, this software helps entrepreneurs to trace their cash-flow and manage their profits on every project. By covering the project management side, this software plays a significant role in the service industries that typically rely on each project's cash generation.

Not only that, but Sage Accounting also applies further enhancements by displaying the best functionality margins for your business. Considering the standard costs, it displays results showing you where money can be saved. Although it requires some input level to generate estimated results, it is more efficient.

As an entrepreneur, if you feel that your business model has more projects and project costs have a vital role in performance, Sage Accounting will help. Even though QuickBooks Online provides an enhanced costing mechanism, as a beginner, Sage Accounting makes the process easy and detailed so you can understand it easily.

3. Xero

With major competitors such as QuickBooks Online, Xero also upholds a prominent reputation in the market. Although resembling QuickBooks in many features, this accounting software has unique features to offer to its clients. Unlike QuickBooks, Xero has more integrated security features that let it leave QuickBooks Online behind. Even though this is the case, Xero lacks many features that QuickBooks offers but can produce plenty of reports, all customized and varying from industry to industry.

It also gives the primary user the ability to create many other users to speed up the operational work. If you are running a small business, you might need more users to log into the software. If your business has multiple divisions on a small to medium scale, then the integrated feature to include people from the different divisions may prove beneficial.

As an entrepreneur, you know everything about your business model. As the market reputation matters a lot, it is essential to know what values your business aims to target. Keeping this in mind, you may want to tap into a new market to spread your business values. Thus, Xero will prove to be the most efficient and cost-effective accounting software to meet your purpose or to meet your particular requirements in such a case.

4. Sage 300

The most advanced use of any software lies in cloud-based systems, where every piece of data is stored and saved. Sage 300 offers the same benefit to its customers by ensuring that every aspect of your business is secured and out of harm's way. The cloud allows your business's financial records to be accessed from anywhere in the world. It has the edge on making sure that your work is streamlined and isn't restricted.

With the standard features, just like Sage Accounting, Sage 300 provides a more secure and integrated line of reporting and maintaining financial records. You may be putting your data and records at risk of being exposed or used by unauthorized users or hackers. Keeping the data inaccessible and not stored on physical hardware at your premises, security is much tighter.

Not only that, but a cloud-based system also allows the information and data to be accessed from anywhere by anyone with permission easily, and it offers a faster recovery time. Invoice generation, payroll, sales, and other facilities make it easier to track any division's performance at any time from any place safely.

5. FreshBooks

Like QuickBooks, FreshBooks has gained popularity, offering various features embedded in its centralized system. FreshBooks allows for full control of the systematic design for you with its consistency and record maintaining abilities. The integration and security features also resemble QuickBooks and Xero. With the integrated CRM and customer track records system, FreshBooks serves all your financial needs.

Being an entrepreneur, you need to know how your customer revenues are maintained and how they can play a vital role in determining your business's goodwill. FreshBooks also offers customer support services to ensure that every client is satisfied and there is no disruption in your company's everyday operations. You must always keep a balanced state of work for both employees and customers as both have a crucial role in your business's success.

FreshBooks offers reliability and consistency, making it a great accounting software for those who wish to have a more precise track record of their customers.

Your business management requires the necessary resources at hand to guarantee a consistent process without any failure or malfunction. Even if you run a small business, you must ensure that where operations are a crucial factor in the business, revenue streams must also be considered to create a more robust business portfolio and its working criteria.

Top Payroll Accounting Tools

As operations grow larger and larger, payroll processing is an essential part of work-related activities. Whether small or large, many businesses use various opportunities to reduce their payroll processing costs and make sure of accurate calculations to avoid any improper payments made to employees. The standard practices that most businesses use are:

- Allowing an outsourcing firm to handle payroll processing
- Making the managers keep track of the team's working hours and reporting it
- Hiring an independent third party who tracks and records employees working hours
- Creating an HR (Human Resource) department that checks the payroll

These methods and techniques are useful and beneficial, allowing many business owners to save necessary resources (either time or cost) and keep everything in order. Even as an entrepreneur, you can easily save time and cost without investing so much money with payroll processing software.

1. WagePoint

A comparatively simple and easy tool to use, WagePoint provides all the essential benefits and uses of payroll processing software. By keeping track of the time and the hours charged in its timesheets, WagePoint essentially becomes an easy tool to use. This not only helps you save yourself from the hectic day-to-day work, but it also ensures that every single form is processed correctly.

One of the significant features it includes, just like every other payroll processing software, ensures that taxes and other such deductions are made automatically and accurately. Is it essential for you to know how much tax needs to be paid and the number of salaries paid? If you are a small business and managing all the employees, this software is excellent for you. As a large business, this software might not be up to par as it can't trace any wrongful payment made to the employees. It doesn't provide the audit trail features that enable you to track the entire movement.

But as a small business owner, this software is suitable because of its simplicity in use and ease of understanding.

2. SurePayroll

Following the same features of WagePoint, SurePayroll offers an even more straightforward and easier version to use without advanced tools or mechanisms. This software is typically used by small business owners who prefer to keep things manageable while ensuring that the entire process follows a smooth and consistent method. This software has no advanced mechanism or automatic time tracking system. It does calculate the tax accurately, ensuring you don't face the consequences of incorrect declarations.

Not only that, but SurePayroll also lives up to its name and makes sure that the payroll is completed powered in the most precise manner possible. Without disrupting or causing problems in any daily tasks, SurePayroll provides every sort of report you may need.

Top Time Tracking and Expense Software

When we talk about payroll processing, the core factor that makes your payroll accurate is time. Many of you may already know that time tracking is a significant factor because no business wants to overpay or underpay their workers. The biggest problem with time tracking is that it causes the payments to change even if there may only have been a single-digit error in punching in the time. To ensure that no such errors or mistakes occur, and every process is followed, here are the best time tracking software packages available.

1. TSheets

One of the best time tracking software packages on the market, TSheets gives its users remarkable features and benefits. By creating a dynamic system where tasks and project confusion are minimized, TSheets integrates your employees' best productivity. By ensuring that everything passes through the series of procedures, TSheets makes it remarkably easy to use and becomes top-of-the-line.

It also allows people to track their time no matter where they are in the world and keep the process streamlined for everyone to understand. TSheets is commonly used for QuickBooks Online and Xero, which integrates time tracking with the accounting systems. By optimizing the work task, TSheets provides various alerts and updates about any tasks or projects.

TSheets can be a bit expensive for you if you are trying to save costs as its cost increases for every user added to the system, but to create a better-managed control system on time tracking, then the increase in cost may be worth it for the problems it can solve. Not only that, but the entire data is stored online so you can process the time at the end of each day by confirming whether the same reconciles with the work limits.

2. Expensify

As the name suggests, this software is generally responsible for taking up the record of expenses incurred. With its scanning features, Expensify takes the records of all the receipts at hand. Being an entrepreneur, you may come across various moments when you won't have the time to upload the reports and images of the day-to-day expenses that occurred. With Expensify, this will all be made easy and a hassle-free task.

This software also works on mobiles, which allows the best use and gives you a more up-to-date status of your expenses. This also gives employees and staff convenience to upload their bills easily and create a reimbursable status for those bills.

3. Neat

Working with the same features as Expensify, Neat works in the same manner and allows its user to scan their transaction receipts. The scanning feature of Neat also functions on Mobile Devices or ordinary scanners to take up the financial data and process it. By sharing the information and details with other people, Neat becomes a handy tool to make everyday tasks easy.

Tips to Help You Select Digital Software

As you can see, there are plenty of accounting software packages that everyone around the world uses, but as a small business owner, keep the following in mind:

i. Only use the authentic version of the software as sometimes people try to scam and steal your data through fake websites and fake apps.

ii. Remember to keep a consistent backup of all financial information in a separate place to your software so it can easily be traced back or recovered with no problems.

iii. Never use cracked versions of software - always purchase an official copy. Using cracked software is not only illegal, but you also run a high risk of losing your financial data or, even worse, being hacked. If you lose your data in this way, you likely will not recover it again.

iv. Always have secure login and password on your computer and the software you are using, which will help prevent unauthorized breaches in the system.

v. Have software with a built-in function of audit trail that explains which user entered the system and what changes were made on the system.

vi. Don't ever hesitate to contact the software's customer support as they will provide you with the desired help you may seek.

vii. Be sure always to create a separate user account if someone else wants to access the data but be careful not to authorize them to access every aspect of the business.

These tips are important to learn and note, as many people commonly make these mistakes when using this accounting software for the first time.

Chapter 5: Setting Up the Charts of Accounts

In this chapter, we will look at the practicalities of setting up and using the chart of accounts. We will cover:

- What the chart of accounts is
- How the chart of accounts play a role in your work
- Setting up the chart of accounts according to your needs
- Making sure that the framework stays consistent and flexible

Let's begin.

What is the Chart of Accounts?

Any accountant who knows his stuff and has excellent advisory skills will ask a potential client one question – "What is your business model?" They want to know your income and expenditure, how you categorize them, and where your business is headed. Almost every single qualitative aspect of the real world has been quantified due to accounting. The same case applies here that your revenues or costs and your business assets have been quantified, explaining the overall business model.

This illustration was given to create a better understanding of what your business model can be defined as. Before the working business model of your company, the financial numbers played a significant role. According to their nature, these numbers need to be categorized in a pre-designed framework that integrated the entire system.

Thus, the understanding of the Chart of Accounts comes into being. The chart of accounts is the framework model of your business model's quantified aspects. Every business model has common elements, which are the core basics of accounting. Every business has:

1. Revenue/ Income

2. Expenses/ Costs

3. Assets

4. Liabilities

5. Equity

These are definitive quantified aspects of your business model, which are integrated within the financial framework known as the chart of accounts. These charts of accounts give a straight understanding of the elements that fall under them. For example, revenue is a generalized term or category defining what it means, but for a service industry business, their chart of accounts will define revenue or income as revenue from customers or contracts or Income from Contract clients, etc.

Vital Role of Chart of Accounts

The Chart of Accounts plays a crucial role in the business as these are the main foundations of your financial statements and other reports, which are generated from here on. You may think that the Chart of Accounts can be created on a general aspect with a little difference depending on the company. However, these always vary from industry to industry. They even differ from business to business in the *same industry.* And you need to know what it is and how to set them up yourself.

Besides all this, the Chart of Accounts is often specialized in a new type of industry whose business model doesn't exist right now. For instance, many startup companies' new and innovative ideas drive them to develop new and improved versions of their businesses. The nature of that business must be known if it is quantified, as it may be a business that doesn't already exist.

Usually, this can be done only by a professional, so understanding how they work is critical if you must do it yourself.

Getting Into the Practical Work: The Chart of Accounts

Before we explain how to set up the chart of accounts, a quick reminder: we will not be going into the details for each software product, but we will explain where it can be navigated from in most cases.

As earlier explained, the Chart of Accounts is a financial framework that quantifies your business model into the financial statements. It is also an indexing system that allows you to navigate your accounting elements with ease. This indexing is mostly considered in number sequences.

1. Assets

The Chart of Accounts mostly starts with the assets. Assets are all those items you may control and receive future economic benefits. These assets start with a number sequence of "1," extended to "1000," where the numbers are allotted as "1000" or "1010" or "1020". This "1000" series is commonly allotted to current assets of cash in hand or cash in the bank, commonly called *Cash* and *Cash Equivalents.* Current assets also include stock in trade, accounts receivables, Deposits, Prepayments, and other receivables. If your business is a service industry, you may not need to set up the chart of accounts for inventory as you may sell services rather than goods.

The "1000" series is allocated as a whole sequence to current assets, which will probably increase. This all depends on you because you are responsible for setting up your chart of accounts, but it does explain standard market practices. If you don't need a particular Chart of Account, you need not include or create it on your list. This entire process is subjective and depends on your requirements.

Fixed assets of Non-Current assets typically have a life span of more than one year and provide benefits over the years. In setting up the chart of accounts of fixed assets or non-current assets, they are allocated to the series sequence of "2000", which can be "2000 for Land and Buildings", "2010 for Vehicles and Automobiles", "2020 for Office Equipment and Furniture" etc.

2. Liabilities

The term liabilities are amounts we owe or simply the obligation by us to pay. In the Chart of Accounts Framework, most liabilities are given the sequence of 3, which of "3000 to 3999". Standard market practices create a considerable gap between each series. This is because new elements or forms of interpretations from the IFRS (International Financial Reporting Standards) or GAAP make it difficult for business owners to consider them immediately. This allows ample room to re-continue with the series with no disruptions.

In the Liabilities series, both current and non-current liabilities are placed in the "3000" series, with current liabilities range from "3000 to 3499" while the non-current range is from "3500 to 3999" series. There won't be that many liabilities in most cases, but for instance, in the banking sector, most of the money the bank holds for its customers is a liability. Couple this to interest income for customers and other benefits, making a big part of the liabilities. For them, a more extensive series sequence would be needed to accommodate the liability headings.

As explained, it all depends on your requirements regarding how you are willing to set the accounts out as these are the market practices, not regulatory requirements.

3. Owner's Equity and Equity Accounts

Owner's Equity sometimes takes a large share as it can include share capital, preference capital, reserved earnings, general earnings, etc. This series can start right after liabilities, which means in the "4000" series. Owner's equity can have variable account types in it, but it mostly covers the entire "4000" series to stay on the safer side of the functioning framework.

4. Revenue/ Income

As we advance, the series moves to revenue or income. You must remember that the revenue or income series is the business's primary revenue or income earned as part of its main operational activities. This revenue series is followed and allotted the "5000" series.

Revenue and income can be of many other types as well. For instance, it can also relate to other income earned, not as part of the main operational activity but as a side or secondary income source. This type of income is recorded under the "7000" series as it differs from primary revenue.

5. Expense/ Cost of Revenue or Sales

Assigning numbers to the accounts in the chart is easy, but the series must differentiate them to address those accounts properly. Expenses can be classified into different types. For instance, Expenses can be Costs of Sales/Revenue, Administrative expenses, Selling and Distribution expenses, or even the Finance Cost Expense. It is essential that each heading is separately identified and given a sequence too.

The series sequence that immediately follows the primary revenue is the Cost of Revenue or Cost of sales, given the series number of "6000 to 6800". This series has to be continued directly after the revenue series as it allows easy identification in the chart of accounts and the financial statements.

Other expenses such as administrative, selling and distribution, and marketing are categorized totally in the "7000" series. This can vary from range to range as some standard practices have a series gap of 300 or 250 before the other expense is started, and most practices just categorize the entire expense in these heads.

Make Your Decision Based on the Chart of Accounts

Regardless of how standard practices are followed, you must remember that you have full control and decision in making your own set of accounts. The real reason a standard technique should be followed is because of the consistency and similarity that allows another person to understand it easily. For example, if your business expands in the upcoming future or in the coming times, you might need to hire an accountant. That accountant must find it easy to understand the framework and the business model to adapt to the work environment and the working criteria. Common practice creates an elaborate but easy understanding of the fundamentals.

The numbering in the series doesn't matter because you can decide the number series at your own will, but the element flow should be followed in the aspects defined above. In software where the number indexing is still followed, these techniques will help a lot.

In QuickBooks Online, Xero, and other software, the number indexing is already pre-defined in the system. We are just responsible for creating the category names from our financial framework. Most software's Chart of Accounts can be navigated from the list option displayed in the upper menu bars or displayed in the company option in the upper menu bars.

Key Fundamentals to Make Sure of Consistency and Flexibility

From going through the process of setting up the Chart of Accounts, you may find that navigating the options is easy. There are things you should remember to make sure of consistency and flexibility.

• Make sure that you can adequately navigate your way around the option on your digital accounting software.

• It is an excellent approach to first draft out a rough format of the entire business model to understand your business model's quantifiable aspects. This will not only save time but also allow you to understand your framework.

• Don't forget to check out the pre-designed formats or sample company accounts present in the digital accounting software, as they will allow you to save time and edit only those aspects you require.

• During the setup process, remove account titles that don't relate to your business model. If your business is a service industry and supplies no goods, then having an account named inventory or stock in trade serves you no purpose.

• Keep things simple and easy to navigate. People can create a complicated chart of accounts that serves no purpose. So always keep everything simple and manageable and only to the extent of your needs.

• If your business model has future diversification expectations, avoid adding accounts that are not followed at earlier stages. Ensure that you only add those accounts you need and show your framework and financials appropriately as too much information or too much of the wrong effort can sometimes result in losing out on valuable resources.

- A wise decision is always to create many series so new heads of accounts can be added later on when the time comes. Give flexibility to your entire process so any change can be easily accounted for and doesn't cause a waste of resources.

Chapter 6: Transactions, Ledgers, and Journals

This section of the book will be more descriptive and provide accounting information and knowledge you need to understand these concepts:

- What is a transaction - and if non-financial transactions matter to your accounts
- What journals are - and their various types
- The ledger accounts and how they are used in digital accounting software
- How digital accounting software processes each phase and part of the accounting cycle
- Ideas on mastering the ledger and journal knowledge.

Now let's get started.

Are There Other Types of Transactions?

In the book's previous chapters, we have discussed the financial transactions and gave a little insight into non-financial transactions. By now, you may have understood what a transaction is and, if you look at your business, you may spot a few things that are not quantifiable. Yet, they do directly affect your business operations.

For instance, you have heard that a new law or a new regulation came up, preventing certain operational activities. This new regulation or law can't be quantified in terms of your business, but this regulation's impact directly interferes with your operations. You may ask yourself if this is even a transaction, and if you should account for it. The answer is "Yes" because this impacts your business and its operations. But what type of transaction is it?

These transactions are known as non-financial transactions, which may need to be accounted for similarly to any other financial transaction. This type of transaction is mostly disclosed, but it is sometimes adjusted in our accounts. These are all advanced concepts, and you need not get into that.

Whether financial or non-financial, the transactions are always considered part of the financial statements. And a transaction is an event that occurred in the past and affects the operations.

Journals and Ledgers: What are They?

For starters, Journal is commonly a short form for the Journal Book, which records and maintains all the transactions occurring in a day or a sequence, the latter of which may be chronological. And any record written in it is known as a Journal Entry.

Journals are the most basic and common forms of record maintaining. In small businesses, people have a book where they record every transaction which occurred in a day – this is the Journal Book. Journal Books are used for cash records and to maintain all the cash-related activities such as making a sale or purchasing an item. Each Journal Book represents a particular account for which the record is entered and maintained. This is known as a ledger.

A ledger is the representation of a particular account that shows the entire movement in it. Journal and Ledger are almost the same because a Journal Book has different types, such as Sales Day Book, Purchase Day Book, General Journal, and Petty Cash Book. All these represent a particular type of account, and these particular accounts are considered ledgers. Journal and Ledgers are the same, but the difference is some journals only record one side of the transaction of an accounting system in it, either as a debit or a credit side transaction. Ledgers record *both sides.*

Start with Journal Types

As a small business owner, you may already have a system where you record all your financial transactions. This could include books where you recorded your sales, purchases, and other cash transactions, with each book serving a specific purpose.

The same concept follows here that the Journal Book has these types:

      i.   Sales Day Book
      ii.   Purchase Day Book
      iii.   Cash Book
      iv.   Petty Cash Book
      v.   General Journal
      vi.   Purchase Return Book
      vii.   Sales Return Book

All these books have specified purposes; let's take a look at each.

1. Sales Day Book

The Sales Day Book records all the credit transactions that occur when selling goods or services to the customer. These books record all the sales made on credit that occurred in the entire day and then create a total amount of the credit sales made to the customers. These books have a standard four columns in which serial number, description, invoice number, and the total amount are recorded. These books can also be customized according to your needs.

2. Purchase Day Book

Unlike the Sales Day Book, the Purchase Day Book records credit type transactions on purchasing goods or services. The total purchases that occurred in the day are recorded here and kept in chronological order. With the same standard format of four columns, purchase day books easily allow the entrepreneurs to keep track of their liabilities.

3. Cash Book

The Cash Book is the prime basis of the ledger formations. The cash book records all the cash transactions that occurred during the entire day or specific period. The Cash Book has both sides of the common T-ledger accounts: a debit side and a credit side. It is recorded on the cash book's left side whenever cash is received, meaning its debit side. It is recorded on the credit or right side of the Cash Book whenever cash is spent.

The Cash Book became the first-ever foundation to the ledger accounts as both sides of a ledger account has a debit and a credit balance to balance out the accounting equation. There is one major loophole in the cash book: when an asset is purchased, it is considered an expense, and it is written on the credit side of the cash book. And when loans or other financing are taken from the bank or any other financial institution, it is a liability recorded on the debit side as cash received. Accountants are careful when examining the cash book because they are looking for various assets and liabilities.

The Cash Book commonly has a two-column type that records the cash at hand and cash at bank transaction, but sometimes the petty cash is also recorded in the Cash Book, which then becomes a three-column type Cash Book. These columns are defined by the various other cash accounts being recorded in the same Cash Book.

4. Petty Cash Book

The Petty Cash Book is the same as a Sales Day Book or Purchase Day Book. It records all the petty expenses which were incurred during the day. Sometimes the petty cash Book is merged with the same central Cash Book and is called a three-column Cash Book.

5. General Ledger

The general ledger records all such transactions that didn't involve cash and excludes all sales and purchases. When the term "sales" or "purchases" is used, it refers to the common sales and purchases made in the current business practice., which can be different depending upon the industry. For instance, a watch-making industry would record sales of watches and purchases of the dials and the glass frame.

The general ledger acts as the dual entry accounting system where it records a debit and a credit, as mentioned before in the previous chapters. Examples of the transactions recorded in this book include credit purchase of a vehicle, depreciation charged on the assets or bad debts, etc.

6. Sales Return Day Book

This book records all the customer sales returns and typically those to whom credit sales were made. The cash sales return is recorded in the cash book, but the credit sales return is recorded in the sales return day Book.

7. Purchase Return Day Book

The Purchase Return Day Book is the same, just like the Sales Return Day Book, Sales Day Book, and Purchase Day Book, but it maintains the suppliers' purchase returns records. It only records credit purchase returns made in a day as the cash purchase returns are recorded in the Cash Book. It also has four columns in total that are the same in the Sale Day Book or the Purchase Day Book.

All these Journal Entry Books are also known as the Books of Prime Entry. This is because these books record and maintain all the financial records at the initial stage of the accounting cycle, the recording phase.

Being an entrepreneur, you may need to use these books as well because they have various advantages.

- These books help keep the entire record in physical form in chronological order
- All records maintained in these books are based on receipts or bills
- These help in accounting for all events that occur daily and as part of the reconciliation processes
- Whenever the auditor requires the details of the transactions, they can also find them in the records present in these books

What Differentiates a Journal from a Ledger?

A ledger is one element of an account containing debits and credits. The real concept of ledgers came into effect from the cash book which small business owners used to maintain.

In a cash book, the left side represents how much money is received and when. Thus, when an asset increases, it is represented as a debit. Similarly, the cash book's right side represents all the cash payments made during the entire period, represented as a credit because it is credited when an asset decreases. This is how the common T-ledger concept came into effect.

To illustrate what a T ledger is, please have a look at the image.

Debit			Bank A/c	Credit	
Date	Particulars	Amount	Date	Particulars	Amount
Jun-19	To sales	80,000	Feb-19	By purchases	45,000
Sep-19	To accounts receivable	30,000	Aug-19	By rent	12,000
			Oct-19	By other expenses	22,000
			Dec-19	By balance carried to balance sheet (balancing figure)	31,000
	Total	1,10,000		Total	1,10,000

The T-ledger has a left side, the debit side, and the right side, the credit side. Now a T-ledger represents one single account. For instance, it can represent a cash account, a vehicle account, a bank loan account, etc. This makes it completely different from the journal because some journals accommodate a single effect, either as a debit or credit.

What Purpose Does the Ledger Serve?

Ledgers are the final entry books that show the dual entry accounting system. It is the start point when all information is appropriately classified and recorded in its relevant headings. Each ledger heading describes separate categories of the account. To prepare financial statements, each heading's closing balance is used after a certain period.

Ledger balances such as income and expenses have to be grouped in the profit-and-loss statement, and they have no opening balance. Ledger headings such as assets, liabilities, and owner's equity do close, but their opening balances always exist in the next period. Being an entrepreneur, you have to extra careful to make sure that every relevant ledger heading is correctly classified into the accounting element. Otherwise, your accounts would be mismanaged and improperly disclosed.

The ledger serves variable other functions such as:

- It ensures that all relevant transactions are accounted for in their appropriate headings.
- It detects any errors, which may arise in calculating the closing balances of each ledger's headings.
- It maintains consistency in preparing reports and other such documents in the later stages when all accounts are closed for the period.

Post Entries on the Ledger

Entrepreneurs must learn every single aspect of their business. Sometimes, you may also spend hours trying to understand an insignificant point and trying to work out the answer. While trying to understand your business's financial aspects, you may feel confused or worried, especially when you understand the dual entry system.

How is a double entry formed?

Go over this section as often as you need to, ensuring you understand it thoroughly. Posting in Ledgers means that when the double entry of a transaction is made, it is recorded in the heading where it belongs. The confusion at this stage is because:

a. You may create or pass a wrong double entry, which will corrupt the information.

b. You may pass the double entry correctly but post it on the wrong side of the ledgers.

To mitigate the first error, the double entries will be explained below.

Debit	Credit
Assets	Liabilities
Expenses	Income
Drawings	Capital

This concept was explained earlier. Naturally, some account elements are found on the debit side, while some are found on the credit side. While performing double entry, you must remember how transactions would represent each element of the account.

For instance,

I.Expenses Dr.- When we incur expenses or when expenses increase, it is debited.

-        If the payment made is through cash, then Cash at hand or cash at the bank would be credited. The reason is that when we pay an expense, our cash gets reduced. When an asset decreases, it is credited.

a. Cash in Hand/Cash at Bank A/C Cr.

-        If the payment isn't made through cash and instead, we incurred the expense but have not paid, it means we must pay later on. It is the company's/business's liability. Here, when a liability increases, it is naturally credited.

b. Liability/Trade Payable A/C Cr.

Similarly,

II.Income Cr. – When we sell goods or provide services, we earn income, and when income increases, it is naturally credited.

-        If the business received the money instantly for performing the services, then our asset, i.e., cash, will increase, and when an asset increases, it is debited.

a. Cash in hand/Cash at Bank A/C Dr.

-        Suppose the customer receives the business's services and doesn't pay the money right away, saying he will pay later. There, it means that the money is due by that person and is the business's receivable. Thus, receivable is an asset on which we have the right, and when an asset increases, it is debited.

b. Receivables/Trade Debtor Dr.

From these explanations, one thing is clear: when certain accounts increase, they naturally show how they correspond, i.e., debit if an asset, expense of drawing is increased, and credit if income, liability, or capital increases. Remember that you can differentiate an asset, expense, liability, income, and capital when accounting and posting transactions by a double-entry system. Otherwise, the common mistake will continue resulting in inaccurate accounts.

The explanation presented eradicates only one confusion. The other confusion, which still exists, is posting the ledger's transactions. For this, always remember that when you pass the correct journal entry, just place the accounts' values on the same side with the other entry's corresponding name.

For instance,

I. Expense Dr.

-       When you pass the entry, you must place the value of the expense on the T-ledger's debit side but must use the account's corresponding name that caused the expense to be debited.

a. If the expense was paid in the form of cash, you must use the name of cash on the expense ledger's debit side.

b. If the expense was not paid and accrued, you must use the name of liability on the debit side of the expense ledger.

II. Income Cr.

-       When you pass the entry, you must place the value of the income on the T-ledger's credit side, but you must use the corresponding name which caused the account to be credited.

a. If the income was credited because of the customer's cash, then the name of cash will be used on the income ledger's credit side. Similarly, the debit side will represent income as the debit side's narration in the cash ledger.

b. If the income was credited, but the customer agreed to pay on a later date, then, in this case, the income ledger will represent the name or receivable on its credit side. Simultaneously, the receivables ledger will be debited with the name of income on its debit side.

These narrations often play a crucial when reconciling the items or tracing transactions in the entire system.

How Digital Accounting Made Posting Easy

Many of you might still feel confused about the entire accounting system. Luckily, digital accounting software made it easy for everyone to use with minimum confusion.

When you provide a service, this digital software generates the invoice on its own once you complete the data. Then it automatically passes the double entry in both of the relevant accounts. The income is credited in the Chart of Accounts, and the other account, cash or receivable, is also debited.

This software has advanced so much that each aspect of the business is automatically handled using the double-entry system. Whether you are buying an asset, receiving funds, or even making an expense, all the work is done automatically, making the work streamlined.

Digital Accounting: Accounting Each Phase

The previous chapter explained what type of digital accounting would serve best for your needs. Now we will detail how this software will guarantee that every procedure runs and performs accurately.

The accounting cycle is far more complicated when it has to be evaluated by the professional accountants on how systems can adapt and respond appropriately. As an entrepreneur, the evaluation doesn't concern you, but these systems' useful functionality does.

The journalism and the ledger formation can become tricky when it is handled manually. Their use can sometimes lead to unknown consequences and errors, which can become complicated and nearly impossible for you to handle. The accounting cycle revolves around the concept of how transactions can be recorded, summarized, and reported, but the far broader aspect of it always starts after reporting.

For most small business owners, the trick isn't to develop a accommodated system that supports your business but enhances your working criteria to make sure things go smoothly and securely. From recording to reporting, everything is easily managed on digital software.

Automatic Transaction Recording and Posting

When you look into the digital systems' recording portion, you will see that from invoicing, managing the cost of sales, asset management tabs to even debt scheduling, etc., everything is present.

I. Revenue

The invoicing system present in each digital software automatically passes the double-entry once we make the invoice. Whether the transaction is cash or credit, the system takes care of the double entry. Not only that, but the track downs would also allow you to trace the payments and when made. Once payments are made, the system only asks for the amount and invoice against which the payment was received. Afterward, the system automatically books the double-entry by reducing the receivable and increasing the cash in the account.

II. Cost of Sales and Expenses

The systems also incorporate all the bills received from the suppliers, whether they are cash or credit. Once the bill is recorded in the system, the double entry is done automatically, including payment of the supplier's invoices.

III. Assets

Most popular digital systems like QuickBooks have an asset management program that records all the assets and passes their double-entry system on their own once purchased on cash. For an asset's credit purchase, the general entry would have to be passed manually.

IV. Liabilities

The common liabilities of trade creditors, i.e., suppliers, are recorded in expenses, but bank loans are not included. This can also be incorporated into double entry automatically. This can be done from the banking tabs present in the digital systems.

Automatic Summarization and Reporting Transactions

Since the system automatically performs all the recording and posting work of the transactions, it can easily summarize all the ledgers and prepare the trial balance. Not only that, but it can also produce various reports for every user's needs.

Chapter 7: Processing Payroll and Taxes

This chapter will go over the essential ideas and concepts regarding business taxes and employee taxes. Let's get started.

What is Business Tax and Is It Different?

You may already know fully what tax is and why tax is paid., but the actual question on your mind wouldn't be what benefits tax has, but rather how your business manages its taxes and stays aware of the ever-changing laws.

You must remember the first essential rule in the business world: the owner and the business are two separate entities. The reason is that the Companies Law or Ordinance (depending on your business function) demands that both, i.e., you and your business, be considered two different entities. In law, the terminology used for "person" includes businesses and companies considered artificial persons.

This is done to evaluate taxes on different bases. Most individuals pay different amounts of taxes to their respective authorities because every person has different income sources that fall under different tax calculation rates. The same case applies to businesses. According to their business model, many businesses have different tax rates and tax amounts, which helps everyone evaluate appropriately.

Thus, business taxes differ from regular taxes that a person pays, and this type of tax is levied on your business's single or various sources of income.

How to Manage Various Types of Taxes

The two major types of taxes, which your business must handle will include:

- Tax-related to Business operations
- Tax-related specifically to payrolls

There are other forms of taxes, but only these two types of taxes shall be mentioned to keep ideas and topics consistent and straightforward

1. Tax-Related to Business Operations

Tax-related to business operations technically involves all the taxes directly or indirectly levied upon the business itself. This doesn't mean it will only include the income tax. Income tax is levied upon the turnover and net profits before taxation, but there are other forms of taxes such as:

I.**Property Tax** – Tax levied upon the commercial building if owned.

II.**Sales Tax** – Tax levied upon the sale of goods or services.

III.**Value Added Tax** - Tax levied upon the goods or merchandise to increase its cost.

Property tax will be charged if you own any commercial building, and the business itself must pay this tax if the business has the property under its name. For instance, in the US, the S-Corp, i.e., Small Business Corporation, is a separate legal entity and can own real estate and other assets. The Sales tax is levied upon the provincial, state, or even federal government's orders on the sale of goods and services. Sales tax typically varies a lot depending upon the customer as different rates apply in different regions. For instance, in India, there are different sales tax rates for some states.

While managing your operations as a businessman, you would have to manage these taxes. They are different taxes, and the consequences of each are different in the eyes of the law. Many people consider that income tax is the only tax they are responsible for paying. However, these taxes must also be managed when taking income tax into the business's growth perspective.

2. Tax-Related Specifically to Payroll

Payroll taxes are a completely different variable. They are related to the payroll taxes, which the business has to withhold from the employees' payroll when making the salary payment or paid by your business if the contract states that the employer will pay all taxes. These mostly include:

    I.Social Security and Medicare Taxes
    II.Federal Income tax withholding on Salaries
    III.Federal Unemployment tax

These taxes are sometimes paid by the employer, which is you in this case, while other times, these taxes are paid by the employees, and it is withheld from their salary payments.

The employee's salary typically plays an essential part in the business because you would have to calculate the amount of tax every month of each employee before paying them. And this will be especially needed if you have three or more employees as this can become a burden if left unmanaged.

Your business needs to keep up with the new employee benefits and payroll taxes as they are ever-changing. The primary responsibility of tax collection from employees or individuals lies with the business because it provides ease in the government's work.

Nowadays, managing business taxes and employee payroll taxes can be tricky when running all its significant aspects. However, many businesses have been able to keep up and maintain their business and taxes through digital systems. Digital systems like QuickBooks, Xero, and others have made things easy, opening doors to vast new opportunities that entrepreneurs can explore.

Processing Payroll on Your Own

Your goal is just like any other businessman's goal: lowering costs to increase profits. Processing your payroll is one way to accomplish this. There are many types of payroll software to make this job easier, so you can sit back and relax.

1. Set Up the Payroll Functionality Manually

Setting up the payroll manually can be a time-consuming task. Still, if you believe that your business model won't integrate with the pre-defined payroll functionality, you can have the payroll features setup as per your needs. Since most digital software has an open feature to allow manual setups and manual edits, you will find using them beyond satisfactory.

I. Select the Payroll Software

For more information about payroll software is the best (and which should be avoided), please refer to chapter 4: 10 Tools for Digital Accounting. That chapter elaborates on requirements that best suit your business model.

However, when selecting the payroll software, you must remember whether you want a centralized digital system or a decentralized system. The payroll service providing software rarely is centralized and differs entirely from the main accounting software. Thus, it is essential that when selecting a payroll software, you select that software best for you and saves you time.

II. Add Your Employee List

The second step in payroll tax processing is to make sure your employee list has complete details with complete documentation. Before you can even create a payroll, you need to have employees introduced to pay the salaries. Details regarding employees can include name, address, social security number, employee identification number, the national identity card number (SS# in the US), working hours, salary, etc.

Suppose you are uploading the information for the first time. There, you will face no issue other than the time consumption factor, but if you already have a payroll service available and are looking to shift, this will cause serious problems as you would have to add all the data employees all over again.

III. Set the Payroll Tax Parameters

Once you have completed all the documents and input the employee list, the next step is to navigate the employee payroll section to create a manual setup. In this setup, you will find various tabs asking you for various information regarding the employees, work, and yourself.

Afterward, you must create the manual tax deduction and allowance charts to perform an automatic process. After this, you will need to ensure that the account's relevant heading is mentioned where the payroll tax liabilities will be credited. For instance, if the payment has to be made to the Federal government under the Federal Unemployment Tax Act (US), you need to mention the authority's name that will receive the tax.

Similarly, once this is done, you must enter the new rates and other tax rates applicable to the employee's payroll.

IV. Organize the Due Dates

This step involves setting up the dates for each payment type, which will be made based on your business. These dates include salary payments, tax payments, and other such payments, etc. You must know and understand the dates on which you must make various payments.

V. Track Time and Record It

Once everything is set up, then it is time to put your operations into motion. Input or allow automatic time tracking software to track the working hours of the employees. This way, you won't even have to enter the time or punch the time in the timesheets manually.

You could also manually enter the time, but that will be time-consuming. Many payroll software and even accounting software offer the automatic time tracking feature and records the time worked in the weekly timesheets and simply wait for your approval.

VI. Automatic Tax Calculations

If you selected the most popular accounting software on the market, you're in luck. QuickBooks will perform automatic tax calculations on your payroll and simply report the amount you must pay your employees. QuickBooks helps you focus more on your business.

But suppose you selected software that doesn't automatically calculate payroll. There, you must spend additional time each month to calculate payable salary to employees. Much online software doesn't even offer automatic tax calculations, which make your day-to-day tasks challenging and frustrating.

Not only that, but the automatic tax calculation software will also withhold the income tax payable by the employees to the federal government.

VII. Pay the Taxes and File Your Business Returns

If you have software that calculates all the taxes payable by your employees and tax payable by your business (on income), you'll have an easier time during tax season – all year round! If you keep updated software (rules and regulations), the program will complete such entries within moments; you only check for the correct amount payable (which the software will provide if timesheets or salary is entered), and you are finished!

Many software products have manual payroll, and, as such, you'll have to perform those tricky calculations yourself – every pay period. Choose your payroll software (or entire software package carefully, ensuring that automatic functions cover all the calculations, not just a few.

2. Outsource Your Payroll

The smartest approach, which many business owners and accountants use, is outsourcing payroll. Different areas of a business, including the support departments such as IT services, HR Department, and bookkeeping, can be easily outsourced while managing your costs. The perfect balance between time, resources, and costs is always achievable by outsourcing the work.

Whether you are just starting your business or running your operations for some time, payroll service providers will get your job done - a real timesaver.

Choose Your Service Provider

When you choose your service provider, consider these three things:

- How much is it going to save you?
- How efficiently will the task be managed?
- How good is their customer service?

I. Upload Your Employee List

Before setting up your employee list with the service provider, you need to ensure that all the documents and related information regarding the employees are complete. If you are using the service providing software for the first time, you will find uploading the information and documents relatively easy and quick.

However, if you switch from your current package to a new package, you must go through the process again. When selecting a payroll service, choose carefully; otherwise, you may end paying considerably more rather than saving a few bucks.

II. Tracking Time and Hours Worked

Many software products support a single device or a single computer that uploads time and tracks hours worked; this keeps other employees from uploading their time on other systems. However, some newer and improved software versions automatically track and import time from the employees' work environment interface. These automatically detect and track time, allowing employees to focus on their work while the software notes every activity from the background.

You may find this software more beneficial because it detects and records every activity. You simply approve or reject the time tracked on the systems.

Once all the time has been uploaded and recorded, you can import all the data at each month's end to reconcile with the number of hours each employee worked.

III. Processing the Payments and Taxes

The final step is automatic, where the service provider keeps track of every single liability and processes the payroll payment for the employees. Besides this, they also process the tax payments for the relevant authorities.

A Key Point When Processing Payroll and Taxes

A few crucial points and critical tips for avoiding untoward consequences include:

- Many people rely heavily on software, and reliance on technology is good, but you need to be mindful of what you input when tracking and auditing your system.
- You need an accountant to perform an audit sometimes regarding the system's operation because this will help you see the more accurate picture.
- Remember to select a trusted software product with fantastic reviews for customer service; you'll need a responsive resource if something goes wrong!

- Your system functions just like your business; it will demand time to learn and implement, so expect that.

- Remember to keep a physical record of every single payroll processed and reconcile it regularly with the system so you can spot any discrepancies.

- Always remember to have a check and balance procedure in place to avoid major mishaps.

- Ensure all the documentation regarding payroll is available early because taxes must be paid.

- You need to keep up with the ever-changing laws and consult an accountant when you feel unclear about the law.

- Remember to check all the business taxes, which apply to your business income sources. Sometimes, new forms of taxes can be levied by the government, so ensure that you are well informed.

As an entrepreneur, you may find that your business's core areas can be managed independently. Still, you need to know that a consultant from an accountant is there to help whenever you face any issue (or anything that seems unclear).

Other forms of taxes need to be managed from time after time, but you might never have to face these as a small-medium owner. Ensure that your business is also registered with the relevant government entities - check state and local laws.

Chapter 8: Financial Statements

Let's look at the importance of financial statements, including an in-depth explanation of income statements, balance sheets, cash flow statements, and owner's equity.

Financial Statements: What are they?

When you run your own business, you want to know how it is performing at any given time, and you can assess this by looking at your business profits or losses. When a business is said to be healthy, that tends to refer to the number of customers or average sales per day.

Financial statements are the summarized form of the entire business affairs and performance for a particular period. They are those reports that allow you and other third parties to assess your business. For most business owners, financial statements are the ultimate objective of understanding how the business operates in a year.

To assess business performance, typically, the prime indicator is the profit or loss statement, which is now called "Statement of Comprehensive Income." This statement is primarily the document that concerns you and your business partners and investors. However, the profit and loss statement only defines its revenues and how it manages its assets and other liabilities. For this, other statements are in place to solve the concerns which many investors have.

Financial statements are the most important business document for any company because almost everyone relies on these reports and uses them to make business decisions. If you apply for a loan, the commercial banks will ask you for the financial statements before considering your application, as will any other credit company you apply to.

Start with an Income Statement

Every business earns income and has expenses and, each year, these are tracked in the financial accounts to allow for accurate reporting. The profit and loss statement (or income statement) consists of the following account headings:

- **Revenue** - this is the principal activity of the business for which the company earns income

- **Cost of Sales or Cost of Revenue** - considered the costs incurred to earn the business's principal activity's revenues

- **Gross Profit** - Calculated when we subtract the cost of revenues or sales from the primary revenues. Gross profit margin plays an essential role in assessing whether the company's operations are earning or losing money on each sale. If the gross profit margins are negative, meaning the company is losing on every sale of goods or service, it means that the company may soon shut down its operations.

- **Administrative Expenses** - Admin expenses mostly include the expenses, which indirectly relate to the operations. These expenses include the office, accounts department, IT department, HR department, and other office expenses. These are categorized separately in the profit and loss statement under the other operating expenses.

- **Selling and Distribution Expenses** - selling and distribution expenses include all those relating to delivering goods to the customer or any commissions related to the sale. This is mostly found in the manufacturing industry, where the goods are distributed to regional branches and sold.

- **Marketing and Advertising Expenses** – Operating expenses, marketing, and advertising expenses include advertising, promotion, and sales commission. Along with that, it also includes the salaries of the marketing and advertising department.

- **Finance Cost** - Finance cost includes all the financial charges and expenses based on paying interest or charges to the bank. This is categorized under *non-operating* expenses.

- **Net Profit** - Net profit is the final stage of the profit calculation, where all the expenses are subtracted from the gross profit. Net profit depicts whether the business can earn a profit after all the indirect expenses related to it. For a business to grow, it is crucial to know whether the business can sustain its operations or grow its operations further, which is determined by this figure.

There are two types of net profit, one is before taxation, and the other is after taxation. The Statement of Comprehensive Income also includes unrealized gains belonging in Other Comprehensive Income, but this is an advanced concept. Before taxation, the net profit gives a partial idea of whether the business can sustain its current economic model.

The taxation expense plays a heavily crucial role as it shows whether the government supports the business function. If the business faces high market instability and higher taxes, the net profit after tax will be heavily disrupted. It will show that no matter how much revenue the business makes, it can never expand while in the current region or country.

This financial analysis, how to read financial statements, and each account heading will be explained in the next chapter. For now, you must remember how the income statement is made.

If you opted to use digital accounting software, the financial statements could be generated instantly with a click of a button; we'll discuss this later.

Balancing the Equation: The Balance Sheet

In the previous chapter, we explained the accounting equation. You may have seen that the accounting equation is always balanced due to the double-entry system, showing an accurate picture of the company's affairs.

For instance, if you are concerned about your business, you will not rely on your business's profit and loss statement, as it doesn't show an accurate picture of your business's strength and value. Thus, you need a statement that shows how many assets your business has to contribute more to the investing activities. Along with that, you also need to check how many liabilities and debts your company has and whether financing options are available.

Similarly, the balance sheet or financial position statement elaborates on the accounting equation and summarizes it into a report.

Thus, the balance sheet or financial position statement gives a more detailed view of the company's affairs. Much of the information regarding assets, liabilities, and owner's equity has been given in previous chapters. Please refer to them to clarify anything you do not understand.

Statement of Cashflow

The statement of cash flows reflects the cash ledger in report format. If the cash method is used for accounting, cash flow would be the entire profit and loss statement along with the balance sheet. If the accrual method were followed for accounting, you would need to create the cash flow statement as third parties will not access your accounts.

Thus, the cash flow statement shows the cash earned and cash spent. The cash flow statement is presented in two forms:

I.Direct method- Where the cash ledger is presented in report form.

II.Indirect method- The statement of profit and loss and Balance sheet is used to report the cash flows.

The IFRS and GAAP promote the use of the indirect method for presenting the statement of cash flow because it sub-divides the entire cash flow into three parts:

- Cash flow from operations
- Cash flow from investing activities
- Cash flow from financing activities

These three parts of the cash flow statements give a more vivid picture of the business's cash flow and show whether the operational activities earn money.

Statement of Changes in Owner's Equity

The statement of changes in owner's equity gives the information regarding the opening equity, the profit and loss for the year, any dividends or drawings made, and the closing equity. The statement of changes also shows the information regarding the owners' capital in the business.

How Digital Accounting Tools Generate These Reports

Even though an accountant is required for an in-depth understanding of these reports, you can get by with a basic understanding of them.

Typically, every accounting software has a built-in report function where the reports are automatically generated. Here, your job would be only to enter the range and the data to extract from the reports. Once you press ok, all the reports will be presented, and almost every single accounting software has accessibility to the general reporting functionalities.

You can also edit these reports manually if you feel heads of accounts are wrongly reported. Simply by downloading the entire report to an excel sheet, you can easily extract and then edit these reports. Note that not all accounting software has these functionalities, but most of these extractions of reports and other downloading features are found in the reports or reporting section.

Some of these digital tools extract reports in other ways as well. Some of them give direct access to various other reports. For instance, if you access the revenue by customer report (if such a report is present in your package), you will automatically access the payment tracks made by the customer. One of the best features of digital tools is that other than principal financial statements preparation, they also facilitate making other reports. For service industries, reports could be like profit and loss per client project, unbilled hours per client, pending reimbursable allowances and expenses, revenue per customer, etc. all these reports allow a great analysis of reports, which will be explained in the next chapter.

Tips to Remember When You Generate Financial Statements

Some general tips regarding the financial statements are:

• Generate financial statements and record entries each month to keep the information intact and secure.

• Financial statements can be easily prepared, but don't give these statements to third-parties without consulting your accountant, as relevant disclosures and other information may be missing from these statements.

• Remember to make sure that your financial statements are the key basis of documents used *in every place*. Don't prepare different sets to submit in different places. This will make information inconsistent and result in fraudulent activities.

- Remember to have a reconciliation check and an estimation check when you are finished preparing the financial statements. This will allow you to see whether the figures reported are accurate.

Even though you and many people try their best to keep information consistent, sometimes, things get out of hand due to time pressure and other issues. So always remember to give proper time to your financial information to keep work undisrupted.

Chapter 9: Analyzing Financial Statements

This chapter will focus entirely on reading the financial statements and how they interpret the information present.

From recording your business transaction events to concluding it on the financial statements, you and everyone associated with your business now just have one concern - how the business performed compared to the previous years and what it means for its future outlook. You might think that your business is at the top right now, but every recorded transaction paints a picture of the previous year. Those who are concerned about the business will estimate and decide the future outlook of the business.

Every transaction you have recorded regarding your business was related to past events. These events have already occurred and been recorded, but potential investors, current investors, and any official body that needs to assess ongoing performance need to understand how the business will grow in the future. For this, top-level investors use multiple techniques, seeking valuable input from your business's performance history, creating a whole scenario in terms of their decision-making.

Can Financial Analysis Give Predictions About Business Performance?

In the stock market, the most prominent trading activities occur over the day, and investors do all these trading activities. From small to medium to even large investors, these investors continuously monitor and observe the stock market patterns and their performance before deciding. These investors sometimes have an expert team of accountants and brokers who work in close coordination all the time. When a deal is ready to be struck, these investors take the chances. However, they assume the companies' working performance and then estimate when they will close their stock market positions.

The exact methods they use, the trends they observe, and the timings all matter to them, and these techniques and methods they use are followed on the financial analysis concept. The financial analysis doesn't involve only checking and comparing figures; it also means estimating the business's trends and patterns.

From the stock market example, you can better understand financial analysis. Any person with basic know-how regarding accounts will also use some of these basic techniques to assess their performance.

Basic Overview: How Financial Analysis is Done

The profit and loss statement shows these elements: revenue, the cost of sales or cost of revenue, the gross profit, operating profit, profit before tax, and profit after tax. Before you even consider the financial analysis techniques, the P&L should be considered. For instance, the moment you receive the profit and loss statement of your business, you can see, at a glance, what is happening and the potential prospects.

Profit and loss isn't the only thing that defines your business growth. For instance, the real reason behind loss or low profits this year might be higher interest and finance costs. Now it isn't safe to assume that your business won't perform properly or perform the same in the future. The best approach would be to cut out the cost by making more principal payments on the loans to reduce the finance cost. Financial analysis doesn't involve decision-making; it gives a rough comparison or idea regarding the business compared with the previous year.

But for now, let's move on ahead with basic financial analysis ideas and decision-making in some instances.

1. Revenue and Gross Profits

You already know what revenue is and how gross profit is calculated. Now let's imagine a situation - the revenue is $1,000,000 while the gross profit is $455,000. Automatically, you will figure out that the cost of revenue or cost of sales is $545,000, i.e., (Revenue − Cost of Revenue/ Sales = Gross Profit, Cost of Sales/ Revenue = Revenue − Gross profit). What you won't realize is the percentage that represents the total revenue. You might wonder why you would need even to find the percentage, and here's the reality: Many businesses have a fixed percentage change between their revenue and gross profits directly proportional and, which has a minor 1- 3% variation. For you, a gross profit of 45.5% of total revenue may seem like an achievement, but what if another business's just like yours earns 55% to 60% of their total revenue as gross profit? When we compare it like this, it clearly shows there are many or significant inefficiencies that may be causing a high cost of sales.

The reasons may include having more labor force and fewer machines, saving a heavy depreciation cost, or their working techniques could be more efficient than the ones you are using. Some of the common inefficiencies could be:

- Use of high-end equipment, which requires heavy maintenance. Maintenance is related to the revenue projects and is categorized in Cost of Sales or revenue, but it doesn't include significant inspection or replacement of parts as these are assets)

- Lack of labor or personnel. This can also include inefficient use of the labor force. (Labors and other workers who are directly involved in the manufacturing or service providing processes are also categorized in cost of sales)
- Purchase of expensive raw materials or incurring excessive overhead charges

This type of financial analysis allows you to make an industry-wide comparison to see how your business performs compared with different competitors.

Now the actual decision-making is left to you, whether you would change the processes or enhance them according to your business model to increase the gross profit margins. This type of decision solely relies on you, but you must account for every single aspect, such as losing profits, which you might suffer from a change in methods, losing personnel, the cost savings, which will be observed, etc.

2. Revenue, Gross Profit, and Net Profit Before Taxation

Continuing the same example mentioned above, let's say that the net profit before taxation is $200,000, whereas the gross profit was $455,000. If we further break the operating expenses down, we will see that the operating expenses, including administrative, marketing, and distribution expenses, cost $105,000. The non-operating expenses, which include finance costs, are only $150,000. Keeping this in mind, we can see that the operating expenses are only 10.5% of the total revenue of $1,000,000. This is promising for your business because most industry-wide operating expenses range from 10-15% of the total revenue. Whether you are a service or a manufacturing industry, operating expenses can't go much lower than this unless operations are small. However, the finance cost is 15% of the total revenue., which is bad because finance cost shouldn't exceed more than the operating expenses.

If we interpret all this information, you understand that the business's finance cost, i.e., that interest expenses shouldn't be that high. It means that the business is heavily financing itself to keep itself afloat. Not only that, if we see that last year's finance costs were less, it means the business took on new loans. Looking at the administrative expenses, since it represents only 10% of the gross revenue, it means that the business should focus on maintaining this ratio. However, if these costs represent over 20% of the total revenue, then the only way to reduce these costs is by increasing revenues or cut the costs.

It is your decision as to whether (and how) you can sustain the business. The best way to reduce the finance cost is by making larger principal repayments on the loans. Principal repayments on loans cause lower finance costs to be borne by the business. Or the alternative way to reduce the finance cost is by utilizing non-interest options such as investment in the business or business associate's formation. Your decision-making on operating expenses lies solely in cutting costs and increasing revenues in the short term.

3. Net Profit Before Taxation and Net Profit After Taxation

As the net profit before tax is $200,000 and net profit after tax is $120,000, you may realize that taxation also plays a significant role in the profits. From this perspective, taxation is only 8% of the total revenue, but the actual comparison of taxation is never made based on total revenue. It is made based on both net profits before and after tax. The taxation is usually charged on the net profits before taxation. If the tax is $80,000, that means it is 40% of the net profit before tax. This is not good; it means the government or the tax authorities aren't considering the business class. The business taxes shouldn't be over 20% to 25% of the net profit before tax.

Once you interpret this, you will realize that the business model needs to be where the taxes can be saved and costs to run the business are minimal. The government sometimes facilitates the business class by incentivizing them with various investment options. As an entrepreneur or a businessman, you need to look for places where your tax can be saved or reduced. When the business keeps more cash and profits, it incentivizes the business to work more and continue its operations. If that isn't the case, it forces businesses to run on debts or loans, causing even more significant business issues.

However, if we look at it from this perspective that the net profit after tax is 12% of the total revenue, it means that the business has excellent potential to grow in the future. But it also means that for every sale of $1, the business earns $.12 as profit.

Decision-making now lies again with you regarding the reduction of the taxes. Taxes can be reduced only if the business model is aligned with something that the tax authorities incentivize. Business incentives can help keep the business going and prosperous over a few years, making them beneficial to you as you will save more cash and more profits by running the business. Ultimately, this will provide larger returns, more cash, better profitability status, more loans for future operational growth, more significant investments, and higher asset turnover.

You can also take various tax credits that your business can receive from its operation or other miscellaneous activities. For this expert advice and other information, consult a tax consultant or an accountant as they will provide you with up-to-date techniques and ways for you to reduce your taxation expenses.

Financial Analysis: Compare it with the Previous Year

The typical financial analysis that managers and the upper management perform compares the previous years' financial results. Here, the previous years or year is the base year. Every aspect, such as revenue, cost of revenue, gross profit, operating expenses, etc., is compared with the new recent year results. For example, if you ever look at a listed company's financial statements, you will find the director's report to provide these fundamental analyses to their shareholders. The comparisons include the financial results of the previous five years.

You will also compare with the previous year to help you understand and find areas that have become ineffective this year. Usually, these are used to determine whether the costs have increased or decreased disproportionately with the revenue. The comparison with the previous year's provides other insights. For instance,

- The incremental costs are incurred when revenue increases after a certain point
- The cost of running operations to the cost of manufacturing the product or providing the services
- The taxation impact over the successive years

The Complex Analysis: Profit and Loss with Balance Sheet

Even though the balance sheet can be explained in this chapter's introductory overview section, a proper understanding can be achieved only with profit and loss. When these two statements work simultaneously, they reveal a whole new picture regarding the business's performance and future expected affairs.

We explained a few assumptions present regarding the balance sheet from the profit and loss statement. For instance, we explained that the cost of raw materials might have become expensive, increasing sales costs. This also means that our inventory (which is the current asset) will also be higher than the previous year. Another example of this is when we mentioned that the finance cost increased in this year. The main reason could be that either fresh borrowings were taken this year or the interest rates drastically increased. This is related to current and non-current liabilities that non-current bank loans (which won't be payable within the next twelve months) have increased. Or that the current liabilities (which will be payable within the next twelve months) have a drastic increase in their amount, which is interest expense accrued.

Thus, we have shown a few examples of how profit and loss correlate to the balance sheet when seen together. Comparing the balance sheet with the previous year can be helpful. Still, this comparison is almost 90% covered in the cash flow statements, which show all the actual amount of increase or decrease. The comparison we are trying to interpret out of both statements relates to operational decision-making.

1. The Current Ratio and Quick Ratio: Cash Flow Recovery

The key elements, which will be interlinked in the current ratio, will include revenue, cost of sales, accounts receivables, inventory, advances, trade creditors, and other payables. The current ratio is essentially the current assets divided by the current liabilities, showing how much cash will be received and how much cash will be paid in the short run. The essential ratio the current assets and current liabilities should maintain is 2: 1. That means for every $1 liability, there must be $2 assets available to pay it when the cash is received.

$$\textbf{Current Ratio} \quad = \quad \frac{\text{Current Assets}}{\text{Current Liaibilities}}$$

Which is to be maintained in the ratio of:

Current Assets (2): Current Liabilities (1)

The quick ratio includes all the current assets, excluding inventory, divided by the current liabilities. The ratio between them can range from 1.3 to 1.5 against \$1 of liability. These ratio values are considered as optimum amounts for them to be reported on. However, the real analysis of these ratios should be explained.

The working capital cycle gives a lot of info regarding when the cash will be received. Stated differently, all the assets such as inventory and accounts receivable are turned into cash. The main goal of the business is to earn cash – and do it fast. Since many costs are used in inventory manufacturing, the accounts payable stands in the liabilities, which must be paid quickly.

The working capital cycle is calculated with the average number of days inventory over a year, plus the average time taken for customers to pay. Then the average number of days for you to pay your suppliers is deducted.

Working capital cycle = avg. # in inventory number + avg. # A/R – avg. # of days to pay.

The average number of inventory days is calculated when we divide the total inventory by cost of sales and then multiplied by 365. The average number of days customers pay is when we divide total accounts receivables by total revenue and multiply it by 365 days. The average number of days to pay is calculated when we divide accounts payable with the credit purchases and multiply it by 365.

Let's assume the values are 80, 30, and 120, respectively, meaning that it takes an average of 120 days before customers pay, so the company takes loans to survive and pay other necessary costs. This makes cash flow look bad, as the business's cash suffers from poor cash flow – sometimes causing late payments, as well. This increases finance costs, which justifies the business's increased costs in the previous example (basic overview section). The business holds its inventory for a longer time and takes even longer to receive payments to make even more late payments to the suppliers.

This example clearly shows that the business is not doing well and must shut down its operations because it will lose the supplier's trust; it needs better inventory management – and an even better *cash recovery system.*

Let's say that these average days are 30, 10, and 7. This means that the company is paying for costs before the cash was received from the customers. On average, it has a full reserve of another 33 days; clearly, an abundant cash reserve is present with the business. It can easily make payments to vendors while maintaining enough cash to sustain operations for another three years. This raises another question regarding the business's use of cash. When there is an abundant amount of cash present in hand, the business must invest the excessive amount. Cash present in excess shouldn't be kept with the business for long as it won't provide value. Hence, the business must invest the additional amount in various instruments and other assets.

From the above illustration, you have a complete idea regarding how complex financial analysis can become. There are more financial analysis techniques, but they can become complex; this basic understanding is all you need for now.

Chapter 10: Closing Your Books

In the section, we will go over a few of the period-end closing techniques involving:

- Book closure event
- Some preliminary tasks to be done before the books closure event
- Adjusting the affected accounts
- Post book closure events

Let's get started!

Book Closure: What Is It and Why Is It Done?

Book closure (or "closing the book") is when all income/revenue events stop for the period – usually, year-end when owners wish to see the business's performance and affairs. Another instance might be when new federal regulations are announced, or a new budget is applicable.

At this time, books are finalized before being closed to ensure that an accurate picture of the company's financial health is depicted.

Crucial Preliminary Tasks Before You Can Close Your Books

Book closures don't occur instantly; some accounts must be prepared before closing. For instance, revenue and expense accounts are two significant areas requiring attention before being closed and reported. We focus more on the revenue and expense accounts because these accounts have certain events that recur over time, are easily traced, and must be accounted for.

For example, in administrative expenses, one of the most significant expenses is the salary and payroll; all the payments must be made before closing. Since salaries are paid the month after period worked, if this expense is left undocumented, it can disrupt the next period's accounts, resulting in incorrect totals.

Another significant expense – often overlooked - is depreciation. Depreciation is the value that your asset will lose over time due to usage or the allocation of the depreciable amount over the useful life of non-current assets. From this brief definition, it is clear that depreciation must be logged at the end of each year, and this task completed before books are closed. Depreciation is charged on different non-current assets on a different valuation basis. If you are using the digital tools for accounting, you will find sub-programs that automatically detect and charge depreciation on the non-current assets after you approve it. Typically, QuickBooks offers automatic depreciation for assets.

Similarly, some revenues are also not logged at the period or year-end. This typically involves those revenues related to goods sold before the period end but recorded as sales *after* the period. This situation occurs less often in everyday practice, but you'll need to remember that the revenue, in this case, must be logged before the period end or year-end.

Finance costs and tax must also be calculated before the books are closed. In practice, taxation is calculated from post book closure, whereas the finance cost is logged and accounted for before the books are closed. Taxation is calculated later on due to pending changes in the reporting accounts, affecting the tax totals in different manners. The finance cost is always logged on as a payment to the financial institution, but it is never accrued at the year-end. Thus, calculation of the finance cost accrued is crucially performed to ensure that all the information is in line so the financial institutions can reconcile interest they received as income.

7 Steps to Book Closure

As mentioned earlier, the revenue and expense accounts are affected most during the book closure event. During this time, seven steps are followed in the same sequence as described.

1. Pass All the Journal Entries

The first step before closing the books of accounts is to pass the journal entries. By this time, you may have gone through the preliminary process of identifying which heads of accounts are left unadjusted. The first step is to pass all the journal entries, particularly those discussed previously, in the preliminary tasks.

Once the journal entries are passed in the system, it will automatically make sure that all the entries have been accounted for this particular event. Make sure that you also pass the journal entries for any significant estimate. A significant estimate includes any provision for bad debts or provision of an event that occurred after the reporting date (this is just for reference to be used in the next series of the book).

2. Close All the Revenues and Expenses Accounts in the P/L Account

First, you will need to open a new account, which will be named the P/L account. Second, transfer all the revenue and expense account balances into the P/L account. This P/L account will clear the revenue and expense account balances and close them into the profit and loss ledger account. Third, make sure that no balance is left on any revenue or in any expense account. This includes the journal entries passed (posted?) during the process or accruals logged to adjust the balances.

At this stage, you can prepare a trial balance and have all the balances shifted in the trial balance. A better approach would be to clear out all the revenue and expense account balances and then make a trial balance. This will keep the trial account simple to understand, and you can see if all the revenues and the expenses have been accounted for.

3. Close the Balances of the Rest of the Ledgers

Now it is essential that you also close all the balances of other ledgers. For this, you will require no additional accounts. The ledgers remaining after closing revenue and expense accounts would be assets, liabilities, capital, and drawings. These accounts won't close for the year; instead, their balances will continue into the next period or year. That is why all the balance sheet elements, such as assets, liabilities, and owner's equity, have an opening balance. The same doesn't apply to profit and loss items, as they become part of another known as an *unappropriated* profit and loss account.

Once all the remaining account ledgers are closed, their balances are ready to be shifted in the trial balance. It means all the required entries in these ledgers have been passed, and after subtracting the debit side from the credit side of each ledger, a final closing balance becomes available to be shifted in the trial balance.

4. Prepare an Unadjusted Trial Balance

A trial balance is a statement that shows all the closing balances of every single ledger account. After combining the debit and the credit side of each ledger, the resulting trial becomes balanced. The sum of all the debit side accounts becomes equal to the credit side of the accounts. The trial balance also functions as the basis for the accounting equation and the ground foundation for the balance sheet or financial position statement.

An unadjusted trial balance is one in which the journal entries have not been accounted for yet. This includes adjustments to be made by the auditors. In companies, the trial balance is left unadjusted for auditors' adjustments because the auditor will pass some entries to ensure that the accounts represent the true and fair view. Thus, the trial balance is considered an unadjusted trial balance because some transactions are left pending for finalization later.

Once the ledger account closing balances have been taken, they are shifted into the trial balance, where they are checked for the omission, transposition, principle, and other errors. These errors will be explained later.

5. Include the Adjusted Journal Entries

The next step is to include all the adjusting journal entries. These journal entries will include those entries which the auditor might find or any other entry you find missed when the books were closed.

The actual area which the adjusted journal entries target is the post book closing entries, which relate to subsequent events. Subsequent events are those which occur after the closing date but relate to the year being reported. In cases like these, you must assess whether the event must be disclosed or accounted for in the financial statements. Sometimes, events like these appear; for instance, you are closing your books on 31st December 2xxx, and you realize after closing your books that most stocks you invested in are worth ¾ of what you invested initially, meaning you suffered a loss. Now you must disclose this information in your financial statements rather than accounting for it because you haven't sold these investments yet and hope to hold them for a little while longer.

Most of the time, the adjusting journal entries could be depreciation, impairment of assets, revaluation of assets, fair value valuation of stocks or property held as investments, etc. Other than depreciation, all these new accounting terms may seem surprising, but don't worry, these things will be explained later.

6. Prepare the Adjusted Trial Balance

Once again, the trial balance has to be made, but in this step, all the adjusting journal entries must be passed in the unadjusted trial balance, which will cause an adjusted trial balance. The adjusted trial balance doesn't mean it is the final trial balance, as it only contains the adjusting entries. There can be other entries, which will be passed before the accounts are closed.

The book closure date and the date when the financial statements are presented are two different dates. The book closure typically occurs within the one-month time frame after the period end date. In contrast, the business owners decide the reporting date when they wish to be presented with the management accounts (if someone else prepares your business accounts).

7. Generate Financial Statements

The final step is preparing the financial statements, which have been explained in the earlier chapters. These statements will include profit and loss statements, balance sheet, statement of cash flow, and changes in the owner's equity.

Use Digital Accounting Tools to Close the Books

All the steps mentioned before were done to show you how the accounts are closed manually clear*ly.* With the digital accounting software tools, all this is possible with just a button click. Almost every accounting software has a built-in function to close the books. Sometimes, software programs automatically generate reports without closing the books, whereas sometimes they close a particular range while generating reports.

Every accounting software has a period-change or a period-close wizard that performs the book closure on its own. However, the software doesn't close all the accounts' aspects because it can't detect unrecorded occurred events. Therefore, passing the journal entries and preparing the adjusted trial balance will be a task you must perform; otherwise, the software will close the period and close all the balances of revenues and expenses in the owner's equity. Once this is done, it becomes nearly impossible to reopen and pass the adjusting entry later on.

Thus, you should prepare a list of adjusting entries that are left unrecorded or might need amendments. This way, you can fix all the issues or problems later on when reconciling all the work in the end.

Chapter 11: Small Business Budgeting

In this chapter, we will discuss the fundamentals of budgeting. Along with that, we will also discuss:

- Secrets of a successful business
- The powerful tools for budgeting
- The expert view on how to perform budgeting

Budgeting: Secrets to a Successful Business

Most people plan out what they will do in life. Some even have elaborate and creating timing for defined goals they want to achieve. Meeting goals is dependent upon one's motivation to achieve more in the available time given. Our lives are full of examples where we plan out and execute decisions. In a certain way, we all try to plan, organize, and work on things we want to achieve.

Budgeting is a combination of multiple elements involving:

- Planning your goals and targeting time needed
- Organizing your schedule to accommodate steps needed to reach targets

- Availability and allocation of necessary resources to ensure that targets can be reached
- Estimating what percentage of the goal has been achieved

In management studies, budgeting plays a vital role in understanding the business's potential to grow. Budgets work as fertilizers for growing business because the budget layout can define how effectively and efficiently you reach targets and, ultimately, the goal.

These estimations and budgets can't be created by just one person, especially if it is a large entity. The involvement of multiple people from different operations creates a diversified viewpoint in terms of goal-reaching. Let's look at the steps involved in creating a budget.

1. SWOT Analysis or Market Analysis

Different types of market analysis are performed before the budgets are made regarding the business's principal activities. There are specific objectives to these analyses.

a. Understanding the Market

Understanding the market demand regarding the product requires you to estimate it first. This research can be difficult because of the data collection requirement, which include:

- Determining which geographical areas in which the products are sold
- Determining the total number of sales for a similar type of product being supplied in the whole market
- Determining the total market demand present throughout the year
- Learning seasonal demand increases within a year
- Discovering, on average, which product people prefer - and why

This requires immense effort and won't be easy!

b. Analyzing the Opportunities

Once the data is collected regarding the market, it has to meet the next objective: analyzing the opportunities. This task is aimed explicitly at understanding weak areas or qualities not yet introduced into the market.

c. The Potential Threats that can Hinder Growth

Once you understand the opportunities, it is crucial to understand which areas of your business are exposed to threats; you must analyze all the competitors present in the market and how much market share they currently hold.

Once these objectives are met, the SWOT Analysis (Strength, Weakness, Opportunities, and Threat Analysis) can be viewed as a whole regarding how the business can increase its total revenue in the next year. This entire analysis lays the foundation to decide:

- The goal for percentage increase in total revenue for the next year
- The total revenue limit the business can achieve in the next year
- The costs to be incurred to ii, above
- The optimal selling price per unit set for the next year

2. The Internal Procedures Analysis

Even though SWOT Analysis requires that the business's strengths and weaknesses are understood, the reality of whether this can be achieved or not is viewed through internal procedure analysis. This typically involves how much demand can be met with the current sales target. In simpler words: how many units can be manufactured? This involves an extensive understanding of what type of procedures would help achieve this target, the additional costs to bear to achieve this target, and the change in methods to ensure optimized costs.

This, in turn, produces answers regarding:

- The number of units that can be produced by the end of next year
- The production unit limits for the next year
- The additional or incremental costs to achieve the new production limit in the next year
- How costs can stay optimized while reaching a balanced supply limit

3. The Cash Flow Forecasts

Another crucial element of budgeting in the business involves the cash flow forecast. In this, the accounts and the recovery department both decide on how cash recovery can be made faster and optimal. Not only that, but they also plan how much cash they will receive from the customers and how long it will take them to pay their suppliers. These forecasts help the finance department understand where cash can be spent optimally while allowing them to look for areas where unnecessary costs can be cut.

This also involves the additional cost or machinery the production department may need to ensure that the production limit is optimally met. To achieve this, the cash flow forecast also involves bank loans or other forms of loans to be used to meet the cash demand while ensuring that costs associated with those finance are minimal or optimal.

4. Compile Everything for the Budget

After these analyses are performed, the budgets are set to reflect the increase in profits in the next year. The reports received from each type of analysis now allows the levels at which the costs will be optimized while ensuring higher profits in the coming year. The budget includes an entire forecast for the next year regarding every aspect of the business, allowing stakeholders to understand how the next year's targets can - and will - be met.

This process will create/generate the financial statements with the budgeted profit and loss statement, budgeted financial position statement, budgeted cash flow statements, and budgeted statement of equity changes. These financial statements shall be the final form, which will be presented as the conclusion of all the reports.

Once the reports and statements are finalized, every department or person is given a new set of targets they must achieve. They are also given the budget allocated to their heads for the next year.

As an entrepreneur, you will need to assess your budgets. These budgets are always estimates and simple forecasts, stating how the business will perform in the coming times. The key player in this entire process is the owner - doing his/her best to ensure that targets are met every month or quarter for the entire year.

Powerful Tools for Budgeting

Some powerful digital accounting tools perform extensive budget reports based on the information and transactions available for the current year. SAAP and other ERP software (Enterprise Resource Planning) provide projections for growth the business will achieve in the upcoming months. However, one limitation of these types of tools is that they cannot provide realistic opportunities that can be used for the business.

These tools can only compile the information or data given to them, but they cannot create out-of-the-limit reports, which can help you analyze the market status. You may want to save costs and prefer not to use such expensive tools. You can use templates and other forms of budgets that your accounting software will provide. This entire process was briefly explained so you can perform a small level of research and produce useful (and realistic) budgets for the future.

A fair recommendation is if you have a small business with a smaller operation like only one or two offices, use the pre-built templates of Microsoft office or the templates present in your digital accounting software. They can help in creating a valuable but small budget for your business. If, however, you must build a much more extensive budget, consult a more advanced book, or consult with an accountant to help you design the perfect budget and cash flow forecasts for your business.

Expert View Regarding Budgeting

Many experts believe that budgets are the only reason a business can survive in the market. Without the will or motivation for future growth, the future can look dim. The advice every expert accountant provides is that budgets define the organization itself. They also define whether the management or owners are serious about growing the business.

That said, many things affect any business's success; budgets are definitely an essential factor in terms of future growth!

Chapter 12: Three Small Business Accounting Pitfalls to Avoid

In this chapter, we will explain some of the common pitfalls small businesses face. These include the three significant downfalls.

1. Lost Receipts

One of the biggest and most common pitfalls of small businesses is losing receipts. Some business owners forget about the bills and receipts they have received because they are too busy managing other aspects of their work, making sure day-to-day operations are going smoothly.

The best way to manage this issue is by having an online app that takes images of the bills and receipts. Additionally, these apps remind you when you have an expense in the system for which there is no image of a receipt.

2. Poor Expense Tracking

Another major issue which the business owners face is not keeping a proper cash record. Cash is received and spent regularly, and there is rarely time to record where it comes from and where it goes.

The best way to manage this is by making cash vouchers whenever someone physically takes cash; this provides at least a temporary record to help reconcile the account later.

3. Failure to Monitor the Receivables and Payables

Another problem is the lack of records for receivables and payables. The issue is never in the payables (the other party, at some point, will receive their money), but rather, lies is when someone owes you money, and there's no record of the payment request.

The best way to tackle this issue is by keeping a steady record of the receivables and payables, ensuring your cash flow isn't disturbed at any point.

Conclusion

This book has not limited its scope to only the core fundamental ideas of accounting; we've provided the various ways you can easily use digital accounting tools and software to manage your records and financial transactions.

We've shown how you can use the various accounting tricks, management techniques, and semi-advanced methods to keep your business operations working steadily and effectively. Even as a beginner, you can create your budgets and analyze your accounts to get a clear picture regarding your company's performances – and how any investor or accountant would view your business activities.

The book is primarily aimed at entrepreneurs and other small business owners who have trouble understanding the accounts' crucial elements, which third parties such as banks, financial institutions, and investors look at deeply. Not only that, but we have also shown that your operational work, such as payroll, tax, and other activities, can be easily managed with digital software and tools.

We hope you've found this book beneficial as you consider the best ways to account for revenue and expenses in your business!

Here's another book by Robert McCarthy that you might like

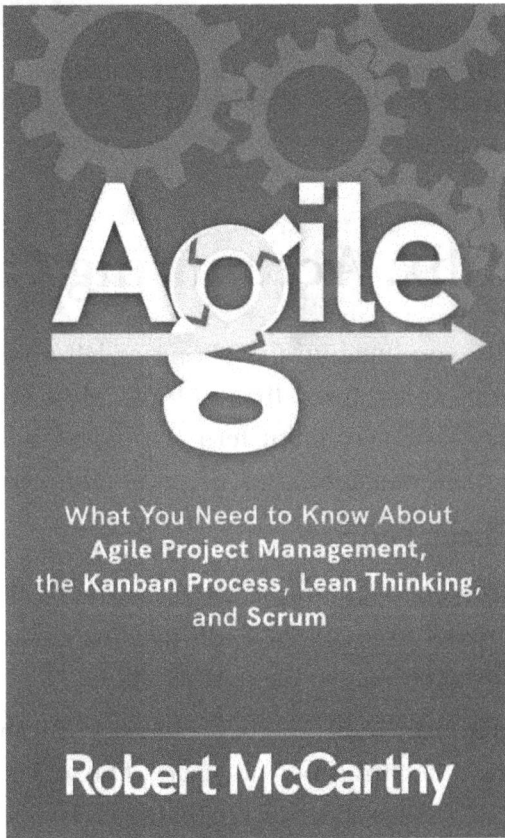

Agile

What You Need to Know About
Agile Project Management,
the Kanban Process, Lean Thinking,
and Scrum

Robert McCarthy

Appendix: Accounting Glossary

How often have you hung up the phone or left a meeting with your accountant far more confused than before? Most of that is down to not understanding the accounting terms, so below is a list of the most common terms, relevant abbreviations, and definitions.

Balance Sheet Terms

Balance sheets are at the top of the pack, the most common of the financial statements an accountant will produce. This section defines the common terms relating to the balance sheet.

Accounts Payable (AP) - The Accounts Payable includes all business expenses incurred but not paid. The AP account is always recorded on the balance sheet as a liability as it is a debt the company owes.

Accounts Receivable (AR) – The Accounts Receivable covers all sales provided by a company that haven't yet been paid for. The AR account is always recorded on the balance sheet as an asset likely to convert into cash shortly.

Accrued Expense (AE) – This is an expense incurred but not yet paid.

Asset (A) – An asset is anything of a monetary value owned by the company. Typically, they are listed in liquidity order, starting with the most liquid, which is cash and ending with the least liquid, such as land.

Balance Sheet (BS) – This is a financial statement listing all the company assets, liabilities, and equity. Its name suggests that it follows an equation – Assets = Liabilities + Equity.

Book Value (BV) – Every asset loses value over time, and this is called depreciation. The Book Value indicates the original value minus any depreciation accrued over time.

Equity (E) – Equity indicates any value left after the removal of liabilities. Going back to the balance sheet equation of Assets + Liabilities + Equity, if you deduct liabilities from assets, the remainder is the equity. This is the part of the company owned by the company owners and investors.

Inventory (I) – This term is used to classify assets purchased by a company to sell on to customers but remain unsold. The inventory account decreases every time an asset is sold to a customer.

Liability (L) – Every debt owned by a company and not yet paid are Liabilities. The most common liabilities include loans, payroll, and Accounts Payable.

Income Statement Terms

The second most common financial statement is the Income Statement, more commonly known as the Profit and Loss Statement. These are the most common terms that relate to it:

Capital (CAP) – This is an asset (financial) or its value, for example, cash. To calculate working capital, you subtract your current liabilities from the current assets – this provides the assets or cash the company has to work with.

Cost of Goods Sold (COGS) – These are the expenses related directly to creating a service or product but, what you won't find here are the business's running costs. Common examples include Direct Labor or Materials in providing goods or services.

Depreciation (DEP) – This is the term used to account for an asset's loss in value over a period. Depreciation can only be warranted on assets with substantial values, and the most common assets are equipment and vehicles. Depreciation is shown as an expense on the Income Statement, normally under the category of Non-Cash Expense. This is because it has no direct impact on the cash position of the company.

Expense (Cost) – Expenses are fees a company incurs and are split into variable, fixed, operational, or accrued costs incurred through a business operation:

- **Variable Expenses (VE)** – expenses such as labor, or any expense that can change within a given period
- **Fixed Expenses (FE)** – payments such as rent that are paid regularly
- **Operational Expenses (OE)** – business expenses that do not relate directly to producing services or goods, such as advertising, insurance, property taxes, etc.
- **Accrued Expenses (AE)** – expenses incurred and not yet paid

Gross Margin (GM) – The Gross Margin is calculated by dividing Gross Profit by Revenue. It shows how profitable, or otherwise, a company is once the Cost of Goods Sold is deducted.

Gross Profit (GP) - This figure indicates whether a company is profitable before taking overheads into account. GP is calculated by deducting the Cost of Goods Sold from Revenue.

Income Statement (Profit and Loss - IS or P&L) - often called the P&L or Profit and Loss Account, it is a financial statement showing expenses, revenue, and profits over a period. Earned revenue is displayed at the top, and expenses are all deducted - the final figure is the Net Income.

Net Income (NI) - This is the amount of profit earned, calculated by subtracting all expenses from each period's revenue. This includes COGS, taxes, depreciation, and overhead.

Net Margin (NM) - This percentage shows a company's profit related to revenue. The calculation is done by dividing Net Income by Revenue for the specified period.

Revenue (Sales or Rev) - Any money a business earns.

General Terms

Lastly are the terms that bear no relation to any specific statement, the general accounting terms.

401k/ROTH 401K - This is a type of savings where employees can put some of their salaries into a retirement account based on the investment. The money is usually tax-free until withdrawn, but employees can continue contributing to their 401K after taxes. Some employers may also match their employee contributions but only to a specified percentage.

Accounting Period - This is designated in every financial statement, including the Income Statements, Statement of Cash Flow, and the Balance Sheet. The period indicates the time reported in each statement.

Accounting Equation - Double-entry bookkeeping that uses the accounting equation of Assets = Liabilities + Owner's Equity or a longer version of it - Assets + Expenses = Liabilities + Owner's Equity + Revenue.

Accrual Accounting – This method of accounting is where income and expenditure is recorded as they are incurred, not at the time they are paid. For example, Sam purchases a book in November but doesn't pay the bill until December. The purchases are shown in the Income Statement in the accounts as being made in November, not in December when the bill was paid.

Allocation – This describes how funds are assigned to each period or account. For instance, costs can be allocated over several months, such as insurance payments or several departments, such as admin costs for companies with several departments.

Business Entity – Often called the Legal Entity, this indicates the type or structure of a business. Some of the more common entities include Partnership, Sole Proprietor, LLC (Limited Liability Corp). C-Corp, and S-Corp. Every entity comes with its own set of tax implications, laws, and requirements.

Cash Accounting – This method of accounting records income and expenditure at the time they are paid, not at the time they were incurred. For example, Sam buys his book in November and paus the bill in January. The income statement will show the purchase as being made in December, when it was paid for.

Cash Book – This is the book where funds are recorded as they move in and out of the company through the company bank account. Every transaction in the cash book should show the following information:

- Transaction date
- Transaction amount
- Description
- The relevant bookkeeping accounts

Cash Flow (CF) – This is the term used to describe cash flowing in and out of a company. Net Cash Flow is determined by subtracting the Ending Cash Balance from the Beginning Cash Balance. If it is a positive number, it shows more cash has flowed into the business than out of it, whereas if it is a negative number, it indicates more cash has gone out than in.

Contra - When a payment is made to an account in the bookkeeping system, and the same payment is then made back out of the account, it is known as a contra. This means they cancel one another out, for example, $300 paid to the Sales account, but the bookkeeper realizes it should have been paid to a different account and pays it back out. Thus, the two payments cancel each other out.

Conversion Balances - When the bookkeeping records are transferred between two different accounting software, it is known as conversion. The closing balance is taken from the original software and entered as the new software's opening balance.

Certified Public Accountant (CPA) - This is a professional designation earned by an accountant after passing a CPA exam. They must also fulfill a set of requirements for work experience and education; these are different in each State.

Credit - Credits are listed on the right side of the double-entry accounting method. Credit entries decrease expenses and assets and increase equity, liabilities, and income. Any money owed by the business to vendors or suppliers is shown as a credit, along with any money owed on credit cards or bank loans.

Credit Entry (CR) - credit entry

Debit - Debits are listed on the left side of the double-entry accounting method. A debit increases expenses and assets and decreases equity, liabilities, and income.

Debit Record (DR) - debit entry

Deductible - This is a purchase a business may claim as a business expense because it reduces the profit. In turn, it reduces how much income tax the business owes the government. Non-deductible purchases are those that cannot reduce the tax and profit, i.e., when the business owner purchases personal items with business funds.

Diversification – This is a common method used to reduce risk by allocating capital across several assets, ensuring one asset's performance doesn't impact the total performance.

Double-Entry – This is an accounting method where every transaction is inputted twice – as both a credit and a debit. The total debits must be equal to the total credits; if not, it is not balanced, and the error needs to be found and corrected.

Drawings – Any money a business owner withdraws from the business for their own personal use.

Enrolled Agent (EA) – This is a professional designation assigned to those who have passed tests in personal and business expertise. Typically, they complete tax filings for businesses to ensure IRS compliance.

Financial Statements – These are reports the accountant produces when the financial year ends. These are based on the financial data the bookkeeper has entered into the system and they show whether a business is making a profit or not. They also show what the business is worth and are used for calculating taxes due to the government, i.e. income tax.

Fixed Cost (FC) – This is a cost that won't change as the volume of sales changes. An example of this is salaries or rent, which do not change when a company sells more or less. A Variable Cost is the opposite of this.

General Ledger (GL) – This shows the entire record of financial transactions for a company. It is usually used to help prepare the financial statements.

Generally Accepted Accounting Principles (GAAP) – These are the rules all accountants must abide by when doing any accounting. The rules were established to ensure an easy comparison of "apples to apples" when going over their clients' financial accounts.

Individual Retirement Account (IRA or ROTH IRA) – These are retirement savings. Traditional IRAs allow an individual to place pre-tax dollars into investments that can be grown "tax-deferred." This means that any dividend income or capital gains are not taxed until the money is withdrawn. In most cases, it is also tax-deductible. A ROTH IRA is not, but some distributions are tax free and not taxable when withdrawn.

Insolvency – the definition of insolvency is "a state where an individual or organization cannot meet their financial obligations with lenders when payments come due."

Interest – This is when a company pays on a line of credit, loan, or mortgage, over and above the principal balance repayment.

Journal Entry (JE) – These are how changes and updates are made to the books. Each entry must have its identifier, the date, an amount, a debit/credit, and a code showing which account has been changed.

Limited Liability Company (LLC) – This is a corporate structure in which each member cannot be held personally accountable for the liabilities or debts a company has. This shields the owners from losing everything if the company were to be sued.

Liquidity – This is a term that references the speed at which an asset can be turned into cash. Stocks have more liquidity than buildings because they can be sold much quicker.

Material – This term is used to refer to whether decisions are influenced by information. For example, if a company has millions of dollars in revenue, a couple of dollars is not material. GAAP dictates that every material consideration is disclosed.

On Credit/On Account – When a purchase is made on these terms, it indicates the payment will be made in time, but the customer takes the product straight away.

Overhead – These are the business-related expenses but only for running the company – they do not include expenses related to making a product or delivering a service, but they include salaries and rent.

Payroll – This account shows all payments made to employees as salaries or wages, bonuses, and any deductions. Shown as a liability on the balance sheet if there are unpaid wages or vacation pay that has accrued.

PAYE – Pay As You Earn, or PAYE is where individuals who earn a salary or a wage has tax deducted at source by their employer. This deduction must then be passed on by the employer to the government, typically monthly.

Petty Cash – Most businesses keep an amount of cash on the premises for small purchases, such as stamps, stationery, etc. This is kept in a safe place, and the bookkeeper must monitor it carefully. The petty cash book contains records of all monies paid out, and this is then included in the accounts. When the money gets low, more money can be given to top it up.

Present Value (PV) – This term indicates the value an asset has on a given day. It is based on a theory that says something is more valuable today than tomorrow because of inflation.

Receipts – This is a document showing payment has been made for something. Businesses produce receipts when they provide a service or product and receive receipts when they pay for a service or other businesses' goods. Received receipts must always be saved so a company can prove the accuracy of its incurred expenses.

Reconcile – This is a process whereby one set of documents or figures must be matched to another. For example, the cash book should be matched to the bank account, and any differences should be investigated and fixed. Another example is ensuring that all the invoices shown on a supplier statement have been received and requesting any that are missing.

Return on Investment (ROI) – This term refers to the profit (return) that a company made on investments. These days, it is a little looser and includes returns on other objectives and projects. For example, a company spent $1500 on marketing and received $3000 in profit. The ROI on what was spent on marketing could be stated as 50%.

Single-Entry – This bookkeeping method is where the financial transactions are entered once, usually within a cash book system. Ledgers and journals are not used for the balancing process.

Trial Balance (TB) – The Trial Balance lists all of the general ledger accounts and their balances, either credit or debit. The total debits must be equal to the total credits, so it is called a balance.

Variable Cost (VC) – Variable costs change as the sales volume changes, and they are opposite to Fixed Costs. They increase as the sales increase because they are expenses related to delivering a sale. For example, a company sells many products and needs to purchase more raw materials to meet demand.

Write-off – If a customer does not pay an amount due, sometimes it can be written off. This entails an entry in the accounts to zero the customer account.

Year-End – This indicates the financial year end and is one of the busiest times of year for a bookkeeper. All the yearly accounts must be finalized and given to the accountant to work out what taxes need to be paid.

Those are the most common terms related to accounting, those you are most likely to come across frequently.

References

Chapter 1: What is Accounting (and Can I Do It on My Own)?

What is an Accountant, and what do they do? By: daveramsey.com
https://www.daveramsey.com/blog/what-is-an-accountant

Why and How to Be Your Own Accountant- The Tools to Use and The
Benefits You will See. By author: Scott Morris
https://skillcrush.com/blog/be-your-own-accountant/

Can I Be My Own Accountant? By: Paypath.com
https://www.paypath.com/Financial-Resources/can-i-be-my-own-accountant

Chapter 2: Accounting vs. Bookkeeping

Accounting and Bookkeeping. By: toppr.com
https://www.toppr.com/guides/accounting-and-auditing/theoretical-
framework-of-accounting/bookkeeping-2/

Accountant vs. Bookkeeper. By: On-Core Bookkeeping
https://www.youtube.com/watch?v=XsMvh4Ygv9I

Top 8 Differences Between Bookkeeping And Accounting. By:
flatworldsolutions.com https://www.flatworldsolutions.com/financial-
services/differences-between-bookkeeping-accounting.php

Chapter 3: Which Accounting Methods Suits My Small Business?

Double Entry Vs. Single Entry Accounting|, which One is Best! By author:
Yaqub Nipu

https://onlineaccountinghub.com/double-entry-vs-single-entry/

Best Accounting Methods for Small Business. By author: Billie Anne Grigg

https://www.fundera.com/blog/accounting-methods-for-small-business

Cash vs. Accrual Accounting: What's best for your small business? By QuickBooks

https://quickbooks.intuit.com/r/bookkeeping/cash-vs-accrual-accounting-whats-best-small-business/

Chapter 4: 10 Tools for Digital Accounting

12 Accounting Tools Every Small Business Needs. By author: Ben Rashkovich

https://www.fundera.com/blog/accounting-tools

The Best Small Business Accounting Software for 2020. By author: Kathy Yakal

https://www.pcmag.com/picks/the-best-small-business-accounting-software

Chapter 5: Setting Up the Chart of Accounts

Accounting For Beginners #20 / Chart of Accounts / Assets, Liabilities, Equity, Revenues, Expenses. By: CPA Strength
https://www.youtube.com/watch?v=yXJVISZA8yU

Develop a Chart of Accounts for Your Small Business. By author: Rosemary Carlson https://www.thebalancesmb.com/develop-the-chart-of-accounts-for-your-small-business-392997

Chart of Accounts- Explanation. By author: Harold Averkamp (Site: accountingcoach.com) https://www.accountingcoach.com/chart-of-accounts/explanation/2

Chapter 6: Transactions, Ledger and Journals

Ledger Account Definition, Format, Types, and Example. By: toppr.com

https://www.toppr.com/guides/fundamentals-of-accounting/books-of-prime-entry/ledger-accounts/

Chapter 7: Payroll, Processing, and Taxes

How to do Payroll Taxes and Process Payroll Yourself. By squareup.com

https://squareup.com/us/en/townsquare/how-to-do-payroll-yourself

Chapter 11: Small Business Budgeting

A Guide to Successful Small Business Budget Planning. By author: Sonya Stinson (Site:

Nationalfunding.com) https://www.nationalfunding.com/blog/small-business-budget-planning/

www.ingramcontent.com/pod-product-compliance
Lightning Source LLC
Chambersburg PA
CBHW050644190326
41458CB00008B/2408